TENT
LIFE

A SLOW LIFE GUIDE

TENT LIFE

An inspirational
guide to
camping and
outdoor living

Sebastian Antonio Santabarbara

FRANCES
LINCOLN

CONTENTS

INTRODUCTION

It's time to get back to basics as we delve into the world of *Tent Life*, a long-standing movement driven by adventurous go-getters, relaxing holiday makers and influential record breakers alike. If you're holding this book in your hands right now and reading this introduction, then the chances are you're already toying with the idea of grabbing a tent and some trail mix before heading off into the woods, your trusty backpack, sleeping bag and maybe a friend or two beside you.

But just what is tent life, and how do we go from canvassing 'how-to tips' on the internet to becoming a champ at setting up camp?

How easy is it to get into camping, and how much money does a person need to spend in order to be able to head out on an off-grid trip along the road less travelled? What's it like seeing the world by bike and canoe, travelling on your own two feet to some of the most spectacular beauty spots scattered across each and every continent?

From the Cumbrian countryside to the heart of the Japanese forests, *Tent Life* covers all aspects of living and thriving in the wild, peeking into the lives of the campers who perch on cliff faces, sleep in tree canopies and voyage deep into the backcountry to kick back with Mother Nature and the animals that call the more peaceful parts of our planet home.

Back in 1996, six-year-old me was having his very first camping experience with one of the contributors featured later in this book. Admittedly, I was still able to go back into my house for a bowl of cereal and my favourite cartoons in the morning, but that very first night in a tent kickstarted a long-standing love of being in the outdoors, living both simply and small while continually striving to find tranquil corners of the wild to dwell in for a night or three.

Since '96, I've had the pleasure of camping in a tree tent in Portugal, pitching up behind a church house in Italy and making camp in the very heart of the Yorkshire Dales, not

to mention ticking off staying over at many of my favourite music festivals right here in the UK. Tent life has shown me how you can make big things happen with very little money or equipment, and that there really is nothing like the thrill of opening a tent flap to watch the sun rise above a glistening lake or cooking hearty meals while basking in the sights and sounds of the forest.

If you've just read the paragraph above and are currently wondering whether you're cut out for building shelters, campfire cooking or off-grid expeditions, then don't worry; you're in good hands. Over the course of this book, you'll hear from people that camp in extreme conditions, people passing on their knowledge of the outdoors to new generations and others who simply enjoy reading a book while the world drifts slowly by.

Since starting this book, I've had the privilege of chatting with tent lifers living off-grid lives on every continent, discovering how they camp, what skills they value and, most importantly of all, what tent life means to them. Throughout each chapter we'll be looking at survival experts primed to thrive in the wild through to weekend campers who live for that morning cup of coffee, covering all the different styles of tent camping and various levels of adventure to suit everyone's lifestyles and exploring abilities.

Don't be fooled into thinking that *Tent Life* is just a book about camping, however. This book serves as a global snapshot of a movement as old as time. It focuses on individuals who are both preserving old crafts and pushing for a change in how the world of camping is perceived on a global scale, setting new standards and goals for the explorers of the future to aspire to while providing travel inspiration to those looking to push themselves to new heights.

And, if you're still on the fence, there are some incredible pictures that will definitely make you want to sell the family car and spend the money on the ultimate tent life set-up.

It doesn't matter whether you're looking to take a trip to the Lakes, planning an endurance trip into the Alps or just fancy a night under the stars with your trail hound curled up at your feet, *Tent Life* will fill you with inspiration and a sense of wonder, all while providing you with guidance from people who live, breathe and dream of all things camping.

1

OFF-GRID EXPLORERS

What secrets lie off the beaten track? For our off-grid explorers, this is the question that matters, the fuel that drives them forward to venture into the wild in search of beautiful locations to reconnect with nature. But being in the heart of nature isn't just something that pacifies the contributors in our first chapter; it's a way of life that calls to them, a need to leave the ordinary world behind and head out into the wild, dropping their problems and stresses at the front door and stepping into a place where they can truly be themselves while discovering, and in some cases relearning, what it means to truly feel alive.

For many, the outdoors also provides comfort, a chance to recharge batteries and release tensions. It's a means of letting go and metaphorically cleaning out the cobwebs, of spending time with loved ones without distractions, of pushing past problems, and of getting to know oneself all over again.

And the best part is, being mindful and in the moment doesn't cost a penny, and come rain or shine, the great outdoors is always open for all.

JACQUELINE

 @rvahikergirl

 USA

Get busy living

 Lanshan 2

When you find yourself hiking for longer and pushing yourself to the limit, wild camping often becomes a necessity in order to recuperate for the next day's adventures. For Jacqueline, however, nature isn't just something she travels through to get from A to B; it's her home, a place that takes her back to her childhood and a time where she felt carefree and at peace with the world. As an adult, tent life makes her feel truly alive, allowing her to relive those childhood thoughts and feelings along the length and breadth of the Appalachian Mountains and all across the east coast of the US, a lifestyle that she jumped into feetfirst back in 2016.

Some people find it hard to relax without the familiar sounds of the city, but for Jacqueline, being alone under the stars with only the trees and animals as company feels simply euphoric, an addictive lifestyle that she can't get enough of. Before setting out on the trail, she carries out plenty of research on the perfect places to camp, heading to YouTube to get information from other campers and the kind of hindsight that you wouldn't usually find on mobile apps or maps. Jacqueline also does her due diligence with regards to wild camping rules to ensure she sets up her tent in the proper designated areas in National Parks, National Forests, seashores, wildernesses and along the many footpaths she traverses.

Jacqueline travels as a solo hiker, a concept that can be quite daunting for anyone setting out on or planning a camping expedition for the first time. Still, she's rarely felt unsafe, relishing trips to remote areas like False Cape at the most south-easterly point of Virginia, a place that can only be reached on foot. If ever she feels a little on edge, Jacqueline makes sure to tell friends and family where she is and who she is with so that people are apprised of her or their location along the way.

When it comes to packing, planning is everything. Jacqueline lays out all her gear so she can mentally tick off everything she needs before weighing her laden pack to see if it's manageable for the distance she's travelling. Whatever the weather, she always packs the ten essential items for camping safety: navigation device(s), food, water, shelter, first aid kit, knife, sun protection, fire making kit, head torch and extra clothing.

With tonnes of life hacks, such as using clothing under her pillow to raise her head for a better night's sleep to packing warm wicking base layers and a liner for her sleeping bag in the colder months, Jacqueline has nailed tent life in the wild down to a tee. With her current plan of section hiking the 2,200-mile (3,540-kilometre) trail between Georgia and Maine fully underway at the time of writing, I'm excited to see the places she'll camp along the way and hopefully one day follow in her footsteps!

THREE ESSENTIAL ITEMS

→ Therm-a-Rest Z Lite Foam Pad – to get the best night's sleep possible

→ Sea to Summit inflatable pillow – because no one wants an achy neck!

→ Helinox Chair Zero – creating a comfortable place to sit no matter the terrain

MOST MEMORABLE DESTINATION

→ The summit of Mount Pleasant in the Blue Ridge Mountains. The incredible sunrise and sunset from the top of that mountain will forever be etched in my mind.

→ If you like the sound of the sunrise over the Blue Ridge Mountains, then consider planning a camping trip to:

    Blue and John Crow Mountains National Park, Jamaica

    Zugspitze, Germany

    Blue Mountains, Australia

AMY KATHRYN

 @bookworm_explores

 UK

Wilderness is a necessity

 OEX Rakoon II

Some people stumble upon adventure, while for others it's been in their blood their entire lives. Growing up with a father who worked as a pilot meant that Amy had many visits to beautiful locations that nurtured her love of exploring, a passion that finally came into its own on a solo trip to Maine, USA. This memorable and somewhat daunting experience found her looking after a group of teenagers in Mount Blue State Park, preparing to sleep on top of a mountain under a simple tarp for the first time, in bear country. A good night's sleep might not be one of the main things that Amy took away from this experience, but her connection to nature and the great outdoors was firmly cemented from that day onwards.

Over time, however, the confidence to head out into the world on her own faded and eventually disappeared. Adventures took a back seat while she pursued a career and revelled in the joys of raising her daughter. It wasn't until Amy connected with members of the Instagram hiking community that she found the courage to get back out under the stars again, trusting in friends to guide her to the beauty of nature and rekindling her faith in the wild once more.

When out on the trail, Amy looks for spaces that are off the beaten track and out of plain sight to erect her OEX Rakoon II lightweight backpacking tent, seeking out places less accessible to others that she must earn the right to camp at, places that also feel safe and not too exposed. Anxiety about being out in the wilderness in any form is perfectly normal, but knowing that she is tucked out of the way helps Amy to sleep much more soundly, preparing herself for a glorious view of the sunrise come morning.

As a self-proclaimed newbie in the camping world, despite successfully navigating 'bear-gate on Mount Blue', Amy is gradually picking up the skills to live wholly off the land from her forest training. Until the time comes when she becomes a bona fide bushcraft expert, she relies on a large 2.5-litre (0.65 gallon) hydration pack and Wayfarer food pouches cooked up on a handy Jetboil, all of which store neatly in her 65-litre backpack.

One thing that Amy takes incredibly seriously is the preparation of her backpack the night before a hike. A first aid kit, snacks, water, changes of clothes, power packs, charging cables and any camping gear are checked and double-checked before being arranged in

'Practise using your gear before you go out on your first trip! Trust me on this one – on the side of a mountain in the dark is not the time to realize you don't know where the poles on your tent should go. Plus, it's fun to camp in your living room as a trial run!'

order of use to cover every eventuality. Although not one to shy away from a sensible risk, Amy checks weather reports before camping and shares her live location with her mother, making sure to leave details of her trip with others back home too, a great tip for anyone wanting that extra peace of mind when out in the wilderness. She never shares her camping location with others via social media, however; another useful piece of advice for staying safe around strangers.

While Amy loves the camaraderie of group camps, she now feels comfortable in her own company once more, relishing the chance to reset in the natural world while soaking up the abundance of free benefits: features that inspire us, help us to grow and provide a literal and metaphorical breath of fresh of air. Going back to basics and living a simple life, finding shelter and watching the wildlife go about their daily business helps Amy to forget about the stresses of the modern world. And as she often says, nature is much cheaper than therapy!

AMY KATHRYN

THREE ESSENTIAL ITEMS

→ Whistle – for attracting attention if you need help

→ Dry bag for storing dry clothes – also doubles up as a pillow

→ Trowel – for burying 'waste' away from the trail

MOST MEMORABLE DESTINATION

→ It has to be my very first experience of wild camping on the side of Mount Blue in Maine, New England. Waking up to see eagles circling the mountain, a wild swim in the lake and fresh blueberries for breakfast is something that I will never forget.

→ If you like the sound of sharing Mount Blue with the eagles and bears, then why not consider a trip to:
Cairngorms National Park, Scotland, UK
The Azores, Portugal
Lofoten Islands, Norway

AMY KATHRYN

ELISE McCABE

Passing on the joy of camping to a new generation

 @elisebilder

 Norway

 Tentsile tree tent

Elise has always had an affinity with camping in the wild. As a young girl, her parents often took her and her siblings into the heart of Scandinavia, camping in a tent beneath leafy bows and the open sky. Now, with her Tentsile tree tent, she is passing on her passion for the outdoors to her family, documenting the joys of tent life through her Instagram @elisebilder.

At the age of eight, Elise bought her very first tent. It might have only been a cheap two-person model, but it heralded unbridled possibilities for adventure without her parents, heading out into the wilderness to discover the world on her own terms. She would often sleep in the forest with her friends, and now she gets to recreate this magic with her own children, uncovering the beauty of nature together.

But rather than taking over an area of the woodland, Elise and her six children become a part of it, listening to the sounds of fox cubs playing or a moose trundling through the trees beyond their camp at night, as though this was as normal as a passing car or a neighbour calling hello. They spend time noting the changing of the seasons and the evolving landscape around the mountains, getting out several times a week to take stock of the things most of us tell ourselves we're too busy to connect with. These moments sitting around a fire or suspended above the forest floor are wholly unique every single time and bring a sense of wonder that can't be bought, paused or replayed at a later date. Life is live, and Elise is savouring every moment of it.

It's this sense of wonder that also drew Elise to a tree tent rather than a conventional model.

As well as providing extra safety from animals that might become a little too nosey when children are around, it's a comfortable experience and one filled with childlike delight. Floating between the trees, Elise doesn't have to worry about uneven ground, rocks or muddy terrain. Once she finds three suitable trees, which given the beautiful Scandinavian woodland isn't a tough task, her Tentsile tent can be erected and ready for camp stories and games in around fifteen minutes.

While it's clear that Elise's love of the great outdoors will never fade, it's the positive impact that this lifestyle has on her children that also drives her to keep exploring new areas and getting out into the wild, no matter the weather. Mastering the art of making a fire and cooking from a young age, as well as building dens and swings, helps them to learn the basic necessities of life while having fun in the world's most exciting playground. It's also a chance to learn about the properties of plants and the names of insects, championing their curiosity instead of hampering it.

And just like Elise did, her children are already taking themselves off into the forest to sleep under the stars, nurturing their own thrill of adventure that will one day be passed down to families of their own. If you ever needed proof that tent life runs in the blood, then Elise's story undoubtedly provides all the answers.

'Pack enough food, preferably food that requires little preparation, especially if you're hiking with children.'

THREE ESSENTIAL ITEMS

→ Wool blanket – for keeping warm on those chilly winter nights

→ Knife – for preparing fires and cooking

→ Torch – for safe exits from the tree tent in the middle of the night

MOST MEMORABLE DESTINATION

→ A place between Haukeli and Røldal in Norway, approximately 1,000 metres (around 3,000 feet) above sea level and about a four-hour drive from where we live. It's a beautiful mountain area with lots of ideal tent sites and peaks to climb. The view is extraordinary, as you can view both the valley (Røldal) and miles of mountains around.

→ If you like the thought of camping in the trees and exploring Haukeli and Røldal, then consider planning a camping trip to:
   Ohře River Valley, Czech Republic
   Isle of Skye, Scotland, UK
   Donner Lake, California, USA

ELISE McCABE

KEV HISCOE

Escaping the digital world and embracing a simple life

 @hiscoe.photography

 UK

 Alpkit Hunka XL

Professional photographer and mountaineer Kev Hiscoe can often be found camping in very heart of the English countryside. You might have seen him bedding down by the side of a trail in his sleeping bag after dark, waiting for the dawn to continue his adventures at first light, or perhaps rallying others to make it to the top of a peak in time for the sunset, a flask of Yorkshire Tea in hand. For me, this is a very special segment, as Kev is the person who first introduced me to tent life back in my grandma's garden when I was six years old. Now, my older and equally folically challenged cousin can be found documenting his many adventures both in and out of the wilderness over at @hiscoe.photography.

Kev has spent his whole life pushing himself in the wild. Dabbling between road life and tent life for many years, he's travelled across both Europe and Australia, revelling in the simple joys of a minimalistic life and living truly for the moment. Equally happy taking himself off to complete the Yorkshire Three Peaks Challenge or heading out on a group hike through the French Alps, Kev feels most comfortable in the great outdoors and knows the value of a warm woolly hat over the latest gadgets or fancy devices.

From camping with his parents to building shelters first with his friends in the local woods and later with the Territorial Army, Kev has had his fair share of outdoor adventures. Now, tent life serves as a soothing release from his high-pressured role as a photographer, giving him a chance to remove himself from diary bookings and email notifications while taking in the ever-changing landscape in which he and I are so lucky to live. Cooking simple trail meals on a portable gas burner and travelling with his tent and bare essentials in tow, Kev much prefers getting back to basics over packing endless camping equipment. In the summer months, Kev sometimes ditches his tent entirely, opting for a bivvy bag or a hammock, waking up naturally with the sun and preparing breakfast for the late risers in his group.

Never one to sit still for long and a constant sufferer of 'itchy feet', Kev has already set himself his next challenge, which is to complete all 214 English Lake District fells listed in the historic Wainwright guides to the area, in the space of a year. With plans to head out to America to continue his camping adventures on the horizon, it's safe to say that I have a fair few family Christmas gatherings listening to Kev's adventures to come in the not-too-distant future. Maybe I'll even get invited on a few for old times' sake!

'Learn how to read a map properly and how to walk on a bearing. Technology doesn't always work on the trail, so having a paper map to hand and understanding how maps work is essential.'

THREE ESSENTIAL ITEMS

→ Jetboil – for making a well-earned cup of tea

→ Head torch – useful for moving around the camp at night but also if the light starts to fail while on the trail

→ Spare batteries – for keeping your head torch topped up at all times

MOST MEMORABLE DESTINATION

→ The Alps, France, snowboarding and camping go hand in hand for me, and I love to get out onto the slopes whatever chance I get. I remember a through-hike where my friend thought we were being chased by a yeti!

→ If the thought of snow sports with a yeti and tent life in the French Alps sounds exciting, then consider planning a camping trip to:
    Mammoth Mountain, California, USA
    Treble Cone, New Zealand
    Ruka, Finland

KEV HISCOE

ABBIE MATTHEWS

 @wanderlustmary

 UK

Always at home in a rucksack

 Vango Banshee 200

Many of us see the great outdoors as simply a place to enjoy some free time between our busy schedules, getting into nature when we can and not fully appreciating how lucky we are to be able to just hike up a hill or traverse a mountain path on a whim. For Abbie, however, the natural world proved a significant lifeline that not only improved her wellbeing, but one that changed her entire outlook on a life that so nearly slipped out of reach.

After being diagnosed with fibromyalgia aged twenty, Abbie was confronted with the prospect of her energy levels receding dramatically, the notion of being wheelchair bound and unable to work an all-too-frightening reality. Rather than succumbing to the inevitable, however, Abbie became more hopeful and determined, working every single day to improve her mental and physical strength and wellbeing. Fast forward ten years, and she has recently completed a near 60-kilometre (36-mile) walk over a 2,750 metres (9,000ft feet) elevation around the Llangollen loop in Wales, proving that there is no mountain she cannot climb or conquer.

It's safe to say that Abbie has definitely caught the wild camping bug (not counting the literal bug she caught while camping when a tick took refuge in her stomach). She is drawn to the mountains as though pulled by a magnet, revelling in the soothing and uplifting experience of lying among the peaks and looking up at the stars, making memories with friends and loved ones that will undoubtedly last a lifetime.

To manage her condition, Abbie has to have the right kit and prepare thoroughly for each and every expedition. She's learned the hard way that carrying too much weight saps her energy and takes the fun out of the camping process. Yet, with her two-person tent and carrying only the bare-essentials and a stash of coffee to hand, Abbie can comfortably trek for hours on end, going further than even she ever thought possible. Before setting off on any hike, she ticks off a checklist of items, filling her 75-litre Osprey pack in a tried-and-tested fashion with vacuum-packed meals, chargers, cooking stove, sleeping bag, hammock and enough water for the trail, as well as water decontamination tablets for if she runs out.

But it's not just for comfort that Abbie consciously packs light. While walking along cliff edges, there have been times where the wind has almost picked her up and thrown her off balance, the added weight of her pack and the elements combined making it difficult for her to stay upright in challenging conditions. She knows more than most the importance of checking her

'The key to a safe night on the hills is to be aware of your surroundings. Research your locations thoroughly, study your trails and always carry a map and compass for when your phone signal fails you.'

more than most the importance of checking her surroundings, researching trails and keeping tabs on the weather, especially when camping so far off the beaten track. Mother Nature can be ruthless at times, and while it's easy to feel invincible, Abbie doesn't leave anything that might jeopardize the fantastic progress she has made with her health thus far to chance.

Abbie spends hours searching Google for beautiful places to visit and areas that boast her favourite natural characteristics – waterfalls and intriguing rock formations – her addiction to being out in nature driving her to pick new and exciting locations in which to pitch her tent as often as humanly possible. For Abbie, tent life is way more than a fad to get bored with after a couple of months before moving on to the next trend; this is a movement that is inherently a part of the resilient person she has become. A health diagnosis that might easily have hampered her movement and self-esteem has instead created a passion for exploring that has turned her life around. Abbie has shown a level of fortitude from which we can all learn something, not least of all the fact that time outside is time well spent, and that with the right will power, we can do anything we set our minds to.

ABBIE MATTHEWS

THREE ESSENTIAL ITEMS

→   Compact self-inflating airbed – for a perfect night's sleep on stones or tree roots

→   Jetboil – because this little burner doesn't set my hair on fire like the larger stove did ... that was a close one!

→   My tent ... and my Contact Coffee pods – a comfortable home-from-home and the perfect place to drink coffee ... what more could anyone want?

MOST MEMORABLE DESTINATION

→   Portree, Isle of Skye. The cliff edges here are simply breathtaking, and soaking in the sights along the Old Man of Storr with my partner and dog is a memory I'll cherish forever.

→   If the cliffs on the Isle of Skye sound exciting, then consider planning a camping trip to:
      Faroe Islands, Denmark
      Capri, Italy
      Kauai, Hawaii, USA

BRENDON WAINWRIGHT

 @brendon_wainwright

 South Africa

Guided by the light of the new moon

 The North Face Stormbreak

A tent is just a weatherproof fort, right? For Brendon, his love for tent life started as a child in the living room, building a makeshift campsite with a tablecloth and pillows. Fast-forward to 2015 and after swapping the tablecloth for his first proper three-person tent, Brendon moved his adventures into the great outdoors, setting out into the beautiful wilderness of South Africa with his friends in tow every new moon to camp beneath billions of stars. From the Drakensberg Mountains to the depths of Namibia, Brendon has sought out some of the most remote places known to camping-kind in order to witness the night sky with as little light pollution as possible, to bask in the infinite possibilities of the cosmos above.

As he's a keen photographer, the position of Brendon's tent for a photo is just as important as it is for a good night's sleep. After checking to make sure the area is safe, he then determines whether any areas are viable for helping to conceal his tent while providing a level and comfortable space to set up camp. Finding concealing features is crucial, as wild camping isn't exactly favoured in South Africa. While the expected behaviour is to visit a designated campsite, it's the challenge of finding suitable locations in the real wilderness that drives Brendon to seek out dry riverbeds and secret nooks hours from the nearest road to be truly away from the rest of the world.

Brendon's camping trips can last anything from two to ten days, the latter being the duration of a trip to the southern side of the Namibia, wild camping all the way. It's this unbridled love of the outdoors that pushed Brendon to pursue a

qualification in mountain guiding, and since 2019 he's been leading budding adventurers up Table Mountain in Cape Town, earning money to fund more new moon adventures for the years to come.

Namibia might hold a special place in Brendon's heart, but it's the beautiful Cederberg Wilderness Area north of Cape Town that never fails to capture his mind and soul, a chance to live in harmony with the wilderness and study it up close and personal with nothing but a pocket full of camera batteries and a head full of dreams. He lives by the motto of 'kill nothing but time, burn nothing but calories', a mantra that the whole world should take heed of to protect both wild camping spots and the planet as a whole for future generations.

'Try and get permission from the landowner and always leave your travel plan with someone who's not on the trip, as well as how long you'll be away for.'

THREE ESSENTIAL ITEMS

→ DSLR camera – for capturing those new moon adventures and the stars from bed

→ Moka Pot – because every adventurer needs a decent coffee to start the day right!

→ Mobile phone – for making and sharing videos, in real time if signal allows

MOST MEMORABLE DESTINATION

→ Cederberg Wilderness Area has a special place in my heart; it's two hours away from Cape Town and it offers really dark skies and some of the most incredible rock formations! I always return there.

→ If you like the interesting rock formations found in the Cederberg Wilderness Area, then consider planning a camping trip to:
Zion National Park, Utah, USA
Fiordland National Park, New Zealand
Waterton Lakes National Park, Alberta, Canada

YUUCA CAMP

 @yuuca_mp

 Japan

Seeking enrichment through the natural world

 Several alternatives

Sometimes the greatest ideas are sparked by simply doing the things we love every day. Yuuca took her love of the outdoors and camping and put it into a new product that has proved both essential for life on the trail and fashionable at the same time. Her 'Little Vest', a short tabard-like garment with pockets and loops for holding camping paraphernalia in an attractive and accessible way, encapsulates everything that she has learnt and wished for while out exploring the natural beauty of the Okubiwako Campground and the Seto Inland Sea, a product that has also struck a chord with the wider camping community, selling out repeatedly in a matter of minutes whenever it goes on sale.

Lovers of both road life and tent life, Yuuca and her husband enjoy the slower pace of life that comes with setting up their portable canvas house and making a comfortable campsite wherever they go. After purchasing a cheap tent from Amazon and falling in love with the lifestyle, she now has ten to choose from, having spent time accumulating the right gear over the years for living the perfect tent life in all four seasons: she can now pick the perfect equipment for every challenge.

It's not very often we notice the subtle nuances that accompany the slow changing of the seasons, but Yuuca's outdoor lifestyle allows the couple to watch the trees change gradually and observe the animals building homes in which to hibernate. They can feel the world around them shifting and evolving, a process that continually enriches their lives. Of the four seasons, winter proves the most challenging. Yuuca knows the value of spending extra money on safety; she rightly fears bad weather and always strives to maintain a responsible camping ethos. After all, it's better to turn back and camp another day than to wake up with frostbite.

Yuuca and her husband adopt specific roles when they reach their prospective campsite, proving that teamwork in the outdoors is a vital part of a successful camping trip. Yuuca lays out the equipment, cooks and takes photos of their trips, while her husband drives, sets everything up and puts it all away, an arrangement that works like a well-oiled machine and one with which Yuuca is more than happy. While they both view solo camping as a lonely activity, Yuuca knows that with her companion by her side, happiness, laughter and an abundance of incredible memories are guaranteed wherever they pitch their tent.

'It is important to have the courage to give up camping in bad weather. You're not being a failure; you're simply being smart.'

THREE ESSENTIAL ITEMS

→ Sleeping bag – for keeping warm and cosy through all four seasons

→ Camera – for documenting our adventures and promoting Little Vest in the wild

→ My husband!

MOST MEMORABLE DESTINATION

→ Hokkaido, Northern Japan. It's the farthest place I can comfortably get to from my house, an area with beautiful large-scale scenery and delicious food!

→ If you like the thought of the sumptuous food and stunning scenery of Hokkaido, then consider planning a camping trip to:
Lausanne, Switzerland
Mount Cheam, British Columbia, Canada
Lisse, The Netherlands

MARTIN HORNSEY

Rediscovering nature through a whole new medium

 @martin_hornsey

 UK

 Hilleberg Allak 2
4-season/trekking tent

Martin first encountered the world of wild camping back in 2018 when he embarked on an adventurous trip into South America and took part in a guided trek through the Andes. As a lifelong fan of travel and exploring off the beaten path, it's fair to say that he was immediately enticed by the lifestyle and wanted to find out more. Imagine his excitement, therefore, at discovering through the help of a friend and the Wild Camping UK Facebook group that the movement had been happening all over his home country without him ever knowing, with fellow adventurers heading out into remote parts of Great Britain to camp in picturesque spots most of the population don't even know exist.

As Martin rightly told me, tent life is all about finding those amazing views, an opinion I'm sure that we'd all share after seeing the scenes that he's experienced on his trips into the wild thus far. For him, spending a night alone on a mountain is infinitely more exciting than clocking into a campsite. On his weekends away, he prefers being able to choose his own spot where he can see both the sunrise and sunset from his tent, going with the spur of the moment and opening himself up to new and exciting possibilities every time he leaves his hometown of Hull and plunges into the natural world.

When heading into remote locations, there's always the chance of getting yourself into dangerous situations. While there aren't any wild animals other than angry cows that could cause a camper harm in the UK, there's always the chance of becoming stranded in bad weather or falling while hiking. Martin always makes sure to let his partner and parents know where he's heading, and follows this with a dropped pin on Google Maps so they know the exact location of his tent and the approximate vicinity of his hiking adventures.

Camping has an initial expensive outlay, but once you've collected the right kit, you can go anywhere, anytime, with zero hassle. From checking out multiple reviews on YouTube and speaking to fellow members of the Wild Camping UK Facebook group, Martin quickly managed to get all the correct equipment to not only complement his adventures, but to keep himself safe, alert and with a full belly on his trips. He never leaves home without his Alpkit Brukit, a completely integrated cooking system perfect for everything from making a hot beverage to whipping up one-pot wonder meals. Each 230g gas canister that the cooker uses lasts Martin around ten camping trips and stores neatly inside his kit, making packing a breeze every time. Swapping between his 4-season Hilleberg Allak 2 tent and trekking pole tent depending on the weather or location, Martin is covered for every possible situation and never lets the elements keep him from getting out and about on a weekend.

'Use a topography map to check the lie of the land before you pick out potential camping spots. Google Maps is also great as people often upload pictures of certain areas.'

THREE ESSENTIAL ITEMS

→ Therm-a-rest Xtherm sleeping bag – an absolute must for staying warm on cold British nights

→ My power bank – to keep everything charged

→ Alpkit Brukit - for hot drinks and food

MOST MEMORABLE DESTINATION

→ I'm going to have to go with the northwest coast of Scotland. It's like another world up there, definitely a place to add to your list if you haven't been!

→ If you like the idea of pitching your tent along the northwest coast of Scotland, then why not consider a camping trip to:
Snežka, Czech Republic
Monte Cinto, Corsica
Feldberg, Germany

TIPS ON BECOMING AN OFF-GRID EXPLORER

1. BOOK YOURSELF A SESSION WITH AN EXPERT

Instead of heading out on your own for the first time with all the gear and no idea, book a session with a trained expert to learn the tricks of the trade. Having someone to teach you how to read an OS map, basic orienteering skills, where to find water and some simple survival skills can really help if things go wrong on the trail.

2. CHECK MAPS OF THE AREA BEFORE SETTING OFF

Study the area carefully before setting off on your journey and acquaint yourself with the lie of the land. If you have an idea about the kind of terrain you're crossing and know where the difficult areas are going to be, you can prepare your route accordingly.

3. PRACTISE USING A COMPASS

Knowing the practical use of a compass just isn't enough; get out there and practise on easy walks with friends, slowly ramping up the difficulty until you're confident that you can find different coordinates.

4. PACK THE RIGHT GEAR

Even when the sun is shining, it's still a good idea to pack lightweight protective gear just in case the elements turn against you. The weather has a notorious habit of changing at the drop of a hat, so always travel prepared. Don't overlook tent life staples like sunscreen, charging units for your devices and enough water for your trip. If you're stuck for what gear to pack, speak to other hikers and campers on social media to find out what they rely on the most.

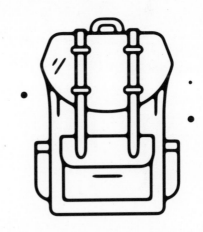

5. GRADUALLY MOVE OUT OF YOUR COMFORT ZONE

Don't jump straight to camping on the Annapurna Circuit if you've only ever camped in your back garden. Rome wasn't built in a day; build up your camping trips slowly and don't bite off more than you can chew.

2

BUSHCRAFT AND SURVIVAL EXPERTS

How many of you would know what to do in a survival situation?

Could you make a shelter out of twigs and twine? Could you light a fire from scratch or forage for your own food? The skills needed to survive in extreme situations are not on most people's radars, and we now live in a world where the concept probably doesn't even cross our minds unless watching a disaster film or driving an unreliable car across a deserted moor.

Truth be told, when I was at school, instead of learning about Pythagoras' theorem or chemical reactions, I wanted to learn how to fend for myself in the wild, to live like my favourite explorers, pushing myself to survive in extreme conditions.

Sadly, this never happened for me, and the closest I got to great outdoor challenges was convincing myself it was alright to eat a sandwich I had just dropped on the ground at a picnic. But, thanks to our next set of contributors, I have rekindled my passion to immerse myself in nature, to mindfully and respectfully use the world around me to thrive in the wild with nothing but my bare hands and the skills to survive. Hopefully they'll do the same for you too.

CAITLIN TIMBER

 @caitlin_timber

 Canada

Thriving in a cabin down by the river

 Marmot Limelight 2/ homemade shelters

We all know the benefits of getting out into the wild and resetting our brains, and for Caitlin, nature provides a means of preventing burnout from her demanding role working for an organisation combatting domestic violence and human trafficking. After a chat with her manager about the benefits of prioritizing her own mental health and the need to fully remove herself from the stresses of her job, she headed out on her first canoe and tent camping trip to Killarney Provincial Park, Ontario. Being in the wilderness allows her to return to her core self, tuning in to her thoughts and feelings and rekindling an awareness of what it means to appreciate the things we take for granted so easily in our overstimulated world: food, shelter and warmth.

Watching her mum single-handedly organize, navigate and lead tent camping trips in the wild normalized solo-adventures, proving to Caitlin from an early age that women can and should feel just as safe and at home in the wilderness as male campers. Now, she's been passing on this sense of empowerment in nature to her daughter ever since her first camping trip aged just seven months. Caitlin tells me that the key to passing on confidence to children while hiking is to lead by example and positive association. If she is anxious and stressed, then her daughter will pick up on that incredibly quickly, but by taking everything in her stride and remaining calm and relaxed, her daughter perceives the outdoors as a fun, friendly and safe space to be.

When not out camping in her Marmot Limelight 2, Caitlin spends her days living in a cabin by the river, surrounded by beautiful forests and a meandering river. She's been placing her daughter in a life jacket in the bathtub from an early age to help her become accustomed to the water, and wasted no time in setting up a play tent in the backyard, taking Caitlin back to the times where she built outdoor forts to play in with her siblings during her childhood. Now, she and her husband have spent countless hours perfecting the art of shelter building for winter camping, a much warmer alternative than camping with a conventional tent and safer, too, when sleeping close to a fire.

Rather than being an inconvenience or a chore, cooking on the trail is something that Caitlin and her husband really enjoy, giving them a chance to experiment with flavours and thinking up new ways to make their favourite dishes in the wild, the most extravagant being a chocolate cake that Caitlin whipped up for her husband's birthday. By throwing fruit and vegetable peels into the fire, they minimize their waste, and they even use frozen meat to keep their other ingredients fresh. With a tinder pouch full of bark and a stack of different-sized sticks on hand no matter where they go, Caitlin can get a good fire going anytime, anywhere with ease.

'Be careful how much you pack. When we first started camping, we used to pack entertainment like cards and books. Now, all the entertainment I need can be found in nature.'

THREE ESSENTIAL ITEMS

→   My ferro rod (fire steel) – for creating sparks to start a fire

→   My knife – for building shelters in the wild

→   Canteen full of water – for keeping hydrated while out on the trail!

MOST MEMORABLE DESTINATION

→   The heart of the Temagami region in Northern Ontario. After a bumpy 25-minute float plane journey, we found ourselves on a gorgeous lake with towering white pines, rocky cliffs, scattered islands to explore, sandy beaches and no other campers for miles and miles. We poured ourselves some wine and relaxed until the plane came back to pick us up five days later.

→   If you like the idea of a relaxing vacation to your own secluded lake, then consider planning a camping trip to:
       Lake Lila, New York State, USA
       Loch Doilean, Scotland, UK
       Lake of Sainte-Croix, France

CAITLIN TIMBER

DENNIS

Skilled bushcrafter passing on experience to the masses

 @5000dennis_nature

 Denmark

 3 × 3 Tarp

Like many children, Dennis was fascinated by the outdoors and spent his time among the trees and delving into caves, making dens and building wooden weapons to fight off imaginary monsters throughout the luscious Danish countryside. He could never have imagined that in years to come, now with a bachelor's degree in pedagogy, he would become an influential figure in the bushcraft world, documenting his outdoor adventures on his Instagram channel as @5000dennis_nature.

It was in 2016 that Dennis first caught the bushcraft bug, finding out about the practice on Instagram, the birthing place of so many current outdoor movements and trends. Instantly connecting with the techniques and skills associated with living in the wild, Dennis sought help from his hunter and fishermen friends, collating maps and tools before beginning his research.

While Dennis enjoys the luxury of a standard tent from time to time, he feels most comfortable using a simple 3×3 metre tarp set up, opting for a Polish Lavvu or a Savotta military tent from Finland, both of which are incredibly durable, can withstand a barrage from the elements and fare well when a campfire is burning nearby. This simple camping set-up keeps Dennis grounded in the heart of nature, increasing his presence in the moment rather than worrying about the stresses and strains of what might be happening in the world outside. And as Dennis has suffered from stress and anxiety in past years, the forest doesn't just provide a place for him to carry out his craft, it is also a place of relaxation and rehabilitation.

Having the ability to create a fire using a bow drill or fire steel means that Dennis can stay warm and dry no matter where he is in the world. The challenge of making camp, finding water, building bonfires and cooking fresh meat using just his skills and the natural resources around him is all part of the magic that drives Dennis and develops him as both a human being and a craftsman. The simplistic nature of crafting with just an axe and a knife has led to him getting creative with building shelters in a local stretch of woodland near his hometown. Paying homage to the tricks of the trade used by our ancestors, he recycles natural materials and continually learns more about the surprising properties of wood as he creates everything from temporary homesteads to cutlery carved from birch and cherry wood.

It doesn't matter whether Dennis is heading away from home for five hours or five days, he always packs a saw (sometimes homemade)

'Make life as simple as possible – everything takes time when you are out in nature, so think about what you want to achieve that day and prioritize your energy accordingly.'

a knife and an axe, the size depending on what crafts he will be carrying out on his journey. A woollen blanket, a pan for coffee and a hand carved kuksa cup to drink from also make the cut, along with other useful items such as a needle and thread, a first aid kit and a water filtration system. Dennis doesn't catch his own food to cook, relying instead on nature to garnish and complement the food he brings from home. With his pan and grate

to hand, he'll look to the forest floor to provide the means for skewering meat to place beside the fire.

Dennis knows that bushcraft isn't a course that you can pass or complete; it's a lifelong experience with learning that continually changes and evolves like the seasons. Like so many crafts, it's not just the equipment that is important, but the experience you accumulate and what you do with that learning that counts the most.

THREE ESSENTIAL ITEMS

→   Knife – for carving and for preparing food

→   Tarp – to create the perfect forest
    living quarters

→   Saw – for cutting wood to make shelters
    and other useful handmade tools for setting
    up camp

MOST MEMORABLE DESTINATION

→   Jutland, Denmark. As I watched the sunset on
    one of my many trips here, I spotted around
    150 roe and fallow deer very close to the place
    I was camping. It was a spectacle to behold
    and amazing to see so many together at once.

→   If you like the thought of deer spotting in
    Denmark, then consider planning a camping
    trip to:
       Wasdale, Cumbria, UK
       Stintino, Sardinia, Italy
       Lüneburg Heath, Germany

CAREENA ALEXIS

Self-taught survivalist championing self-sufficiency

 @alexisoutdoors

 Canada

 Homemade shelters

Harnessing skills picked up from watching her two heroes, Canadian TV-show *Survivorman*'s Les Stroud and bushcraft expert Ray Mears, Careena Alexis began teaching herself the art of bushcraft back in her early twenties. Continually exploring Ontario and pushing herself to learn skills that promote self-sufficiency with her canoe, backpack and white truck to hand, she regularly camps through all four seasons while relying on natural materials to survive in the wilderness.

Bushcraft has a set of principles when it comes to building and placing a shelter. When Careena makes her homemade abodes, she finds a spot in a safe space away from overhanging dead branches or trees that might topple over and ruin her structure in high winds or storms. She maps out a space that is big enough for both her and her gear to fit in comfortably, keeping everything from spare clothes to camera equipment dry and secure no matter the weather. She turns to birch bark rich with flammable oils when it comes to making fires, collecting dry tinder, kindling and logs to maintain a nice blaze for cooking and keeping warm.

Wild camping in the depths of the Canadian forest means coming into contact with animals of all sizes on a regular basis. From smaller critters that chew into food wrappers to bears curious as to who is camping in their territory, Careena has to keep her wits about her to stay safe at all times. She hangs strong smelling food from a tall tree away from her camp when not in use and thus far has never had any issues. Taking her time when

cooking and being careful with spills keeps her camp off the radar of larger animals too.

Like building shelters, cooking on the fly on homemade fires takes some practice. No matter the trip length or the weather, Careena never leaves home without her Finnish knife for any cutting and cooking preparation. She plans her route in advance and calculates how much energy both she and her trail hound will expend over the course of their adventures, packing rations accordingly and adding a little extra in case she becomes waylaid on the return journey. Careena doesn't eat bland meals either, packing steak and sausages for a forest banquet, melting snow or boiling lake water to whip up rice, potatoes and other vegetables to accompany the main event, as well as high fat foods like cheese in colder weather. While canoeing, Careena also enjoys a spot of fishing, later preparing and cooking her catch from her homemade shelter.

Other than her trusty titanium pans, Careena always makes sure to bring a small bamboo toothbrush and zero-waste toothbrush tablets on her trips with her, along with a small bar of natural soap, usually used first to rinse in warm water before she jumps into a crystal-clear lake.

THREE ESSENTIAL ITEMS

→ My favourite Finnish knife – essential for when making shelters

→ Fire steel – for making fires anytime, anywhere

→ Quality clothing/footwear – there's no such thing as bad weather, just bad clothing. Get prepared!

MOST MEMORABLE DESTINATION

→ Algonquin Park, here in Ontario. This is the place I learned to camp and is still one of my favourite places to go on canoe trips!

→ If you fancy learning bushcraft in a place like Algonquin Park, then consider planning a camping trip to:
Bled, Slovenia
Black Forest, Germany
Lake Conasauga, Georgia, USA

ALEXIS OUTDOORS

LAVI AND OLLIE

 @lavi.and.ollie

 Global

Circumnavigating the globe by motorcycle

 Denali Kakadu II

Lavi and Ollie are the perfect examples of when thrill seeking and survival camping combine, pitching their tent everywhere from the Moroccan desert in a sandstorm to chilly nights in national parks as they attempt the challenge of being the youngest pair to circumnavigate the globe on a motorcycle. No strangers to travel, they've spent plenty of time living in a campervan while travelling, tackling a 3000-kilometre (nearly 1900-mile) walk across New Zealand and completing a 2000-kilometre (1242-mile) cycling trip through the UK. Now, with their eyes set on a world record, they're motoring their way across the world and recording every twist and turn of their epic adventure on their Instagram @lavi.and.ollie.

At the time of writing, Lavi and Ollie have pitched their tent around 400 times through twelve countries, including Bosnia and Herzegovina, Australia, Indonesia and Scotland. Their epic nearly 50,000-kilometre (31,000-mile) journey from London is set to take them through thirty-five countries over five continents, eventually bringing them back to their exact starting point two years later. Far from the bustling areas of Hannover and London, Lavi and Ollie now often find themselves sheltering from harsh conditions in arid deserts and seeking out isolated areas with only the wildlife to keep them company.

No longer beginners at the camping game, Lavi and Ollie have honed their packing list down to a tee. As much of their storage space is now taken up with camera and filming gear, they keep luxury items to a minimum and only bring the essentials, with a sleeping and cooking set-up mainly comprising of foldable Sea to Summit items and the bare essentials when it comes to clothing making the cut alongside any snacks they might want to munch on the road.

Meals are usually pretty simple and inexpensive while Lavi and Ollie are out travelling: boiling water poured over dried ingredients and some canned veggies provides all their sustenance. Obviously, in some of the remote locations they pass through, they always make sure to pack a couple of days' worth of non-perishable items in case there's a problem with the bike or they find themselves unable to progress on their journey. Rationing water is essential too, with a 5-litre (around 1-gallon) water bottle lasting them between one and two days and two 2-litre (½ gallon) water bladders extending that time in areas where water is not as easy to come by.

From supporting each other through one of the most demanding journeys of their lives to problem-solving on the go and sharing the logistical nightmares around border crossings, Lavi and Ollie are a tight-knit couple who always have each other's backs. Whether camping behind a police station or trying to snatch a few hours' sleep beneath a mosquito net, as long as they have their easy-to-pitch, lightweight Denali Kakadu II tent and each other, they are confident that they can, quite literally, take on the world.

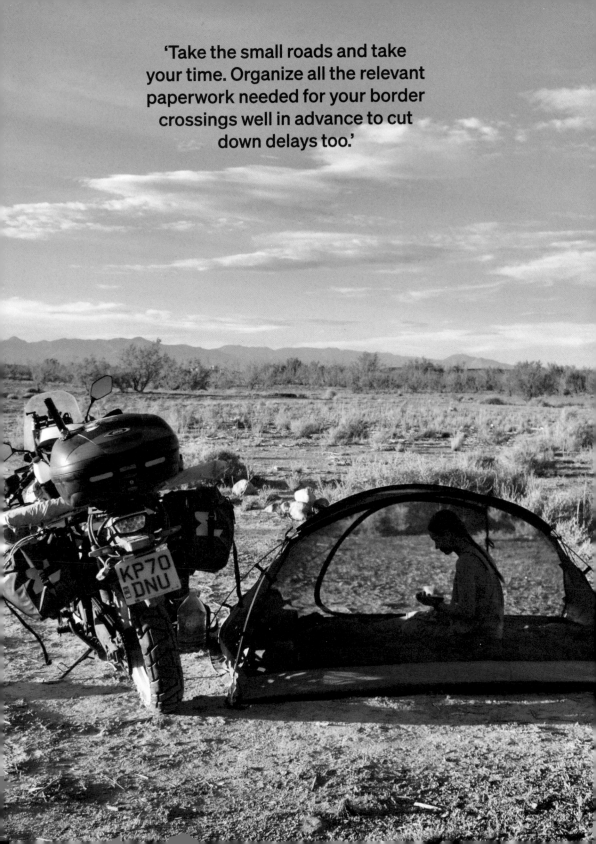

'Take the small roads and take your time. Organize all the relevant paperwork needed for your border crossings well in advance to cut down delays too.'

THREE ESSENTIAL ITEMS

→ Ear plugs and sleeping mask – for getting a good night's sleep no matter where you are

→ Camera – for documenting the journey of a lifetime

→ Kindle – for winding down in the evenings

MOST MEMORABLE DESTINATION

→ Morocco. The land of deserts, mountains and sweet mint tea from local villages. The perfect country for a motorcycle tour!

→ If you fancy heading out into the mountains of Morocco and sampling the local delights, then why not also take a trip to:
Hochwanner, Germany
Vinicunca, Peru
Bohemian Switzerland, Czech Republic

LAVI AND OLLIE

GARETH GREPPELLINI

Outdoor ambassador guiding new bushcrafters

 @ukbushcraft

 UK

 Homemade shelters

Some people might find the jump from working for a large global corporate business to finding themselves in the middle of nowhere using nothing but a small tool roll kit and a head full of survival skills a daunting prospect, but not Gareth. As the founder of @ukbushcraft, an outdoor and adventure company with an aim of teaching others how to thrive in the wild, Gareth's mission to turn his hobby into his full-time job is well underway. He's creating a life where those sunny, carefree days spent in the woods while growing up never have to end.

It was a father–son overnight stay with Woodland Ways, a UK-based company that offers camping trips where visitors build and then sleep in homemade shelters while learning all about outdoor meal prep, that first ignited Gareth's passion for bushcraft. Since that day, he's thrown himself into learning everything there is to know about the craft, practising setting up shelters and making fires in his back garden before being lucky enough to meet his camping heroes out on the trail, making new friends and strengthening both his mental and physical resilience beyond any level that he could have possibly ever dreamed of.

One of the things I love the most about Gareth's work with UK Bushcraft is the food that he prepares in the wild for himself and his guests, all cooked using fresh ingredients and packed full of flavour. Even when he led an expedition to Sweden and lived on a cold and windy island for three days, he still found the time and energy to marinate beef, cook up a curry and make apple crumble with custard to boost morale and fill hikers' hungry stomachs. He's no stranger to a nettle and basil leaf pesto or whipping up pork and trout dishes in a homemade smoker either, proving that even in the middle of nowhere, you can still eat as if you're at a five-star restaurant.

Packing for a bushcraft expedition is something that changes between trips. Gareth adapts his kit list before and after every journey, evaluating which items he uses the most, which he needs for this next adventure and which he could do without carrying. Gareth relies on his bushcraft knife, folding knife, woodcarving knife, knife sharpener, folding saw, torch, multi-tool and fire steel for striking when making fires. He explains that you can never have enough cordage, either the traditional paracord, premium Kevlar cord, or twine made from natural sources such as willow bark. Still, no amount of gear can prepare him for hearing a rustling at night while visiting his makeshift toilet: every caterpillar sounds like a cougar, and even after all this time, those unseen critters still send shivers down his spine!

I've spoken a lot about having a sense of freedom in the wild, and Gareth mirrors this opinion and enjoys the benefits that being at one with the wild can bring. Still, there are times when, whether due to being the pack leader or sometimes just facing the cruelty of the elements, he's felt alone, even when camping with others. This is when a comforting slice of apple pie can go a long way, as can remembering what he's working towards. Being mindful of everything he's achieved helps him to push forward and continue moving from strength to strength.

THREE ESSENTIAL ITEMS

→ Head torch – not just for throwing light on toilet trips in the middle of the night, but for finding your way back to camp and evacuating in an emergency

→ Knife and ferro rod (fire steel) – for striking sparks for a fire

→ Paracord – really useful for putting together structures or for hanging food from trees

MOST MEMORABLE DESTINATION

→ My friend Dave introduced me to an amazing location in Scotland where the Black and White Esk rivers meet. A fabulous camp in a stunning woodland valley, which must be very special when the fish spawn in the river.

→ If you like the sound of camping in Scottish woodland valleys and relaxing by a meandering river, then consider planning a camping trip to:
>   Hannicombe Wood, Devon, UK
>   Mau Forest, Kenya
>   Waipi'o Valley, Hawaii

GARETH GREPPELLINI

FIVE ESSENTIAL TOOLS FOR SUCCESS IN THE WILD

1. SHARP KNIFE

A good knife is a bushcrafter's best tool. Not only is it one of the most-used pieces of equipment in everyday practices when clearing areas and preparing firewood, it's also used for making other handmade tools and parts of your camp. The style and size you choose is a personal decision, but my advice is to spend the money on a good knife that will last you many adventures; you're going to need it!

2. WOODCUTTER'S AXE

If you want to clear an area to make camp in or cut logs into smaller pieces to keep a campfire going, then an axe is certainly going to come in handy. You can use an axe for all sorts of tasks, including using the back of the blade as a hammer for securing poles for your shelter into the ground.

4. ROPE, CORD AND TWINE

Ropes and cords of all kinds come in handy for multiple tasks in the wilderness. Whether using twine to tie pieces of a shelter structure together or rope to hang food from a tree out of a bear's reach, you'll turn to rope for all sorts of jobs. Make sure you have plenty before you head out into the wild.

3. FIRE STEEL

Fire steel is durable, long lasting and creates that all important spark to set your tinder or kindling alight. Holding a scraper or your knife, scrape down the fire steel at the right angle stopping about half a centimetre from the bottom. It takes a little practise, so hone your technique before heading out on the trail.

5. FIRST AID KIT

Cuts and bruises are all part of life in the outdoors. Always have a well-provisioned first aid kit stocked with analgesics, plasters, bandages, micropore, safety pins, rehydration tablets and any other activity-specific items with you at all times.

3

WEEKEND CAMPERS

Do you find yourself counting the remaining seconds on the clock until Friday evening comes around? Is the pull of packing your tent and heading out into the hills so strong that you're already organising meal prep on Wednesday night, and do you prefer sleeping in your sleeping bag to sleeping in your bed?

It sounds as though you are already a weekend camper!

When the weekend beckons, so too do the mountains or the beach, and the chance to leave spreadsheets, emails and phone calls behind, relieving yourself of to-do lists and household chores and putting everything out of your mind until Monday morning.

Don't forget that weekends are also meant for spending time with the family, getting outside and playing games in the fresh air, making memories and sharing incredible experiences.

To quote my literary hero J.R.R. Tolkien, 'the world isn't in your maps and books, it's out there'. So, instead of watching other families doing things in adverts and films, grab the family, pack a tent and think a little more like Gandalf! Who knows what magical weekend adventures you might end up enjoying?

WILD CAMPING WANDERERS

The greatest results come from the greatest challenges

 @wildcampingwanderers

 UK

 Hilleberg Nammatj 2/ Vango Banshee 200

Tent life isn't just about the bond that we share with the great outdoors, it's also about the bonds we form with the people who share in our adventures. For father-and-son team Dougie and Josh, it's a chance to push themselves to the limit, relying on their mental and physical fortitude as well as each other as they seek out breathtaking spots to camp using their trusty tent, capable of withstanding whatever Mother Nature throws at them at heights of over 800 metres (more than 2,600 feet).

Dougie's work and Josh's study calendar mean that the pair only get out into the wilderness twice a month, but that doesn't stop them from spending every spare minute planning their next adventures. Thorough research about their prospective surroundings, for example to find out where the nearest water sources are and which are the safest ledges to camp on, are key to every wild camp. Dougie and Josh have been tested countless times by the elements: snow blizzards, high winds of up to 80 kilometres (50 miles) an hour and, once, a middle-of-the-night evacuation down a mountain in the dark, have all accounted for the level of respect both father and son have for each other, along with the knowledge that they have each other's backs no matter what.

The comfort of the campsite has its place, but for the Wild Camping Wanderers, it's the challenge of wild camping that drives them. They have a penchant for being in control of their destiny, and exercising this in the solitude of the great outdoors provides a thrill like no other. Inspired by the adventures of Christopher McCandless, Alfred Wainwright's books and many YouTube campers

who head out on adventurous expeditions, they try to memorize every twist and turn of their path as well as points of interest along the way, preparing themselves for their next explorative quest.

As well as their battle-hardened Hilleberg tent, Dougie and Josh carry a BeFree filter for dipping into becks and tarns, phones for hiking apps, and a map and compass in case technology unexpectedly fails them. While Dougie prefers Wim Hof's method of ice-cold river washes, Josh favours a wet-wipe wash in the warmth of the tent, leaving his dad to receive questioning looks from passers-by as he fulfils his wild swimming ritual in new and exciting locations around the UK.

While the climb to the summit of their chosen mountain might feel gruelling due to their heavily laden packs, the obligatory fist bump on reaching the summit cairn marks a moment of accomplishment and sweet relief. Once the tent is up, Dougie and Josh set up camp and start whipping up some tasty meals, refuelling to replenish calories spent on the arduous climb. Once full, they kick back and watch the sunset hundreds of metres up, without another soul around. After watching a movie, they'll head back out to study the night sky, relishing the chance to spend quality time together in a unique setting better than any package holiday could provide.

It might be the challenge and the freedom to roam in the wild that initially pushes Dougie to drag Josh to greater heights, but it's the shared experience and lifelong memories made along the way that leave Dougie hoping for many more adventures with his son over the years to come.

'Always prepare for the worst
outcome. It might mean carrying a
couple more kilograms in your pack,
but the weather is so unpredictable
that it doesn't pay to chance it.'

THREE ESSENTIAL ITEMS

→ Eye mask and ear plugs – this sleeping equipment is definitely an integral part of our kit to block out the light and wind!

→ Power pack – it gives us peace of mind that if someone gets injured, we'll always have a charged phone

→ Quality head torches – it cannot be stressed how important these are when alone and up high on a mountain

MOST MEMORABLE DESTINATION

→ Pillar, in the Western Fells of Wasdale in England's Lake District. This 892-metre tall mountain (just over 2,900 feet) is one of the highest we have camped on and the trail to the summit is our longest to date, taking three-and-a-half hours to navigate. We were rewarded at the summit by 360-degree views of Great Gable, the Scafells and Haystacks.

→ If you're tempted by picturesque views, then consider planning a camping trip to:
Pouakai Tarns, New Zealand
Gorges du Tarn, France
Mount Field National Park, Australia

CHICHIFUSION

Outdoorsy family championing quality time in nature

	@chichifusion
	Japan
	Tarp tent in summer/ bell tent in winter

What's the best way to spend time together as a family? While gathering around a Nintendo Switch or snuggling down to watch the latest episode of a series you've all been following can be a good way to connect with one another, there's something wholesome about getting back to basics and truly experiencing each other's company without distractions, uninterrupted by notifications from mobile phones and the other devices we rely so much on in today's world. Chisato and her family value the freedom to have the space and time to have meaningful conversations, actively contributing to each other's lives and spending quality time together as a family unit.

So far, Chisato, her husband Yasu and their two children have camped in over seven regions across Japan, documenting their journeys as @chichifusion. In the summer months, they travel with a two-room tent and tarp, with separate rooms for the adults and children to sleep in. In winter, they swap the conventional tent set-up for a larger model, complete with a wood-burning stove to ward off the bitter chill of the mountains.

With the whole of Japan as their playground, Chisato and Yasu's children have ample opportunities to explore the wilderness around them and to test their strengths when it comes to outdoor living. Rather than being overcautious and preventing their children from learning new skills and trying things for the first time, Chisato always tries to show them how things are done safely in a controlled environment and is always nearby to help guide them when performing new tasks. Similarly, the family always practises how

to put up a new tent together at home, in advance of setting out on a trip, so that everyone feels confident in getting their shelter ready at their new destination. After camp has been set up, the family likes to take off on stand-up paddleboards or play together either in the river or with a SwingLine (a children's toy with multiple swings on it), before coming together in front of a stunning vista and settling down for a well-earned snack.

With their trips lasting only around two days and the longest up to five, Chisato and Yasu bring all their food with them, rather than foraging on the trail. They cook fresh meals over a roaring fire or in an electric cooker hooked up to a portable power pack, making sure that everyone goes to bed with full and happy tummies. Their personal campfire favourites are cheese fondue and skewered cutlets; no one said that tent life food couldn't be gourmet now, did they!

'Social media is filled to the brim with tips and tricks on camping. If you're a beginner, there's tonnes of information here, and it's a great way of documenting your adventures!'

THREE ESSENTIAL ITEMS

→ Fire – for cooking in the summer and keeping toasty warm in the winter

→ Shoes – having the correct shoes for outdoor adventures is essential!

→ Camera – for documenting our travels together as a family.

MOST MEMORABLE DESTINATION

→ A beautiful campsite at the foot of Mount Fuji, a place that we have shared many happy memories as a family.

→ If you like the idea of camping beneath the majesty of Mount Fuji, then why not consider a camping trip to:
 Mont Blanc, France
 Mount Olympus, Greece
 Mount Sinai, Egypt

RYAN FARMERY

 @ryanfarmery

 UK

Finding artistic inspiration in nature

 Halfords dome tent

Often, when we work intense jobs that require a lot of concentration, the natural world provides a sense of release and a chance to step back and take in the whole picture, opening our eyes, hearts and minds to our environments and slowing us down completely. For Ryan, tent life provides a place to stretch his senses, a chance to take in inspiration for his artistic endeavours and breathe the country air all at the same time.

After camping at Download Festival for the first time in 2015 aged twenty, Ryan was soon swapping a raucous evening with Slipknot and Kiss for a relaxing adventure in the Yorkshire Dales with friends, learning, as most of us did, how to put up tents and cook outdoors through sheer trial and error, and making it up as he went along. Now, having had multiple trips to beautiful locations throughout the UK and yurt camping holidays in France, Ryan has found his camping rhythm. His confidence increased, he now heads out in smaller, intimate groups to climb, hike and just generally take a break from his demanding routine.

As a tattooist working on intricate art pieces throughout the working week and often designing until the early hours of the morning, Ryan is more than ready for a chance to kick back with a beer in the heart of nature on the weekend. Far from a professional hiker or extreme camper, Ryan is an advocate for the simpler approach to camping, and that's something he's more than happy with. After all, camping doesn't always have to be about pushing oneself to do more. Rather than forcing himself out of his comfort zone, he's happiest

relaxing in the security of a campsite, knowing that whether taking his bike out for a spin or heading out on foot into the hills, incredible routes and stunning scenery are never too far away. Following signposted trails and leaving complicated navigation to the experts, Ryan simply enjoys being in beautiful locations, never living by an agenda or itinerary and doing what he likes, when he likes.

One of the biggest problems Ryan first faced when heading out on his tent life adventures was

'I know it might seem tough to leave your job behind, but it's important to switch off often so you don't burn out. Leave your job at the door; it'll still be there when you get back on Monday morning.'

switching off from the pull of bookings and the need to answer enquiries, a feeling that many freelance and self-employed workers know all too well. Consciously making the effort to turn off notifications and ignore work are undoubtedly the key to a successful camping session, but social media still plays a big part in Ryan's many adventures. Taking to Instagram, he connects with campers from all over the UK when finding the best trails and places to camp in, subscribing to hashtags for areas of natural beauty that he can visit with his trusty Volvo and camera in hand.

Perhaps due to his artistic background, Ryan finds himself being drawn to the subtle nuances of nature even more than others, something that he captures in his personal photography work. This different artistic release helps him to unwind, to see the world through a fresh pair of eyes and, above all else, remind himself that no matter what pressures he might face through the week, there's always a quiet corner of the world where he can't be reached come the weekend; a little slice of paradise where, for two to three days at a time, his booking diary is firmly closed for business.

THREE ESSENTIAL ITEMS

→ Portable phone charger – for keeping my
phone charged to contact friends/family in
an emergency or for taking impromptu pics
without my camera

→ Barbecue – for cooking up meals with friends
in the evenings

→ Mountain bike – I love to ride, so having my
mountain bike with me means I can get out
and explore further afield

MOST MEMORABLE DESTINATION

→ Cockermouth, Lake District, England.
Exploring along the River Cocker and relaxing
in the quaint market town with a cup of coffee
is my idea of a weekend well spent. Cumbria is
such a beautiful county and there's always so
much to see and do.

→ If you're partial to a quaint towns and lovely
lakes, then why not plan a camping trip to:
Hallstatt, Austria
Annecy, France
Ketchikan, Alaska, USA

WHERE'S MY TENT

Ambitious couple chasing dreams of full-time travel

 @wheres_my_tent

 Ukraine/Netherlands

 Bristol tent

If you're looking for a memorable destination for your first hiking and camping trip, then why not follow in Daria and Mike's footsteps and head to the 5,000 metre-high passes (nearly 16,500 feet) on Mount Kazbegi in Georgia. With it being their first time heading into the wild and much different from their home countries of Ukraine and the Netherlands, however, their first trip was a learning curve that certainly had its ups and downs. With only one sleeping bag and no tent, a romantic night under the stars quickly turned into them seeking refuge in a church tower and waiting impatiently for the sunrise, opting for a quick nap in the mountains on the descent back down to civilization.

Once Daria and Mike gathered the right equipment for the job and did a little more research, they headed back into the great outdoors, thoroughly embracing the world of wild camping on their adventures through fourteen countries, including Kyrgyzstan, Bosnia and Herzegovina, Albania and more, with their longest camping trip lasting thirty-four days. While they always try to find stunning locations to call home, sometimes the simplest spots that they happen upon after a long day of trekking provide the answer. To date, the strangest place they've camped still has to be the middle of a roundabout in Spain, where they awoke the following day beside three other tents occupied by homeless members of the local community who graciously accepted Daria and Mike's gift of their sleeping bags.

As we all know, keeping costs to a minimum and making our money spread further can often be what travelling is all about. Daria and Mike usually try to hitchhike as much as possible, and they eat fresh produce from local markets to make their funds last longer. And, of course, the other benefit of tent life is having free accommodation wherever you lay your groundsheet.

Daria and Mike have certainly seen a lot of interesting and exciting places on their travels since heading out for their first expedition in 2017, though they both agree that being in the heart of nature in areas untarnished by humankind is the best place for their mental health and wellbeing. It's the one time where they can be true to themselves and open themselves up to the unknown, from visits by wild animals to the tranquil rendition of the dawn chorus while looking out at a beautiful sunrise. With no plans to stop their outings across the globe and many more stunning and unusual locations to tick off their bucket list, I have a strong feeling that Daria and Mike will be asking each other 'where's my tent?' for many more years to come.

'Don't walk before you can run. Respect nature and don't take on more than you feel comfortable on your first outing.'

THREE ESSENTIAL ITEMS

→ Inflatable beds – for making any surface comfortable enough to sleep on

→ Tent – the perfect free place to stay no matter where you are

→ Sleeping bag – to stay warm everywhere from lovely beaches to Georgian church towers

MOST MEMORABLE DESTINATION

→ Hitchhiking along the west coast of Europe from Paris to Malaga, camping in beautiful locations throughout France and Spain, and showering everywhere from gas stations to fountains in city centres

→ If the thought of travelling along the European west coast sets your wanderlust soaring, then why not consider planning a camping trip to:
    Tybee Island, Georgia, USA
    Cape Town's Atlantic Seaboard, South Africa
    Amalfi Coast, Italy

THE GEORDIE WILDCAMPER

Reconnecting with nature

 @the_geordie_wildcamper

 UK

 Hilleberg Soulo

Can you remember the first person who introduced you to camping? For Steven, aka The Geordie Wildcamper, he owes his love of the wilderness to his adventurous grandad and their first forays into the wonderful Northumberland countryside. Like many outdoorsy children Steven's age, he went on to join the Scouts to further his knowledge of the natural world, igniting a passion that would see him travelling as far as the Rocky Mountains in North America and the high mountain passes of Ladakh in India.

Like it does for so many of us, however, the responsibilities of adult life soon took over, leaving Steven with less time to get out into the great outdoors. It wasn't until 2020 and the increased pressures of a national pandemic that Steven made a conscious effort to improve his mental health, getting out on a weekend to immerse himself in pure mountain air while challenging both his body and mind. For Steven, wild camping isn't just about beautiful views, it's a chance to find peaceful solitude and tranquillity, to go with the flow of the universe and to concentrate on the here and now instead of the demands of adult life.

Being alone with one's thoughts and relying solely on oneself on a solo camping trip can be quite a daunting prospect. Nervous anxiety leading up to that very first trip can reach fever-pitch all too quickly, but as Steven so rightly explained to me, it's important to remember the lasting benefits that can come from testing yourself in uncomfortable situations. Not only has his mental fortitude and confidence grown, but also his self-belief that he can achieve anything to which he sets his mind. By picking a location he was familiar with and making sure multiple people knew where he was, he had a safety blanket of knowing that help would not be too far away should he need it.

As all wild camping fans will tell you, their equipment set-up is incredibly personal, and the only way to determine what you truly need on the trail is to get out there and to experience everything that nature has to throw at you. Nowadays, Steven relies on his tried-and-tested one-person geodesic Hilleberg Soulo tent, but he's hardly been a one-tent-man over the years, working his way through many different models to hone his set-up. Steven also tries to purchase second-hand gear or recycled items whenever possible too, helping to keep perfectly good equipment out of landfill.

If there's one piece of equipment that Steven thinks encapsulates the slow life ethos, it's his alcohol stove. Not exactly known for its quick food prep times, the process of both setting it up and cooking on it is methodical, from putting all the elements together, blocking the wind, pouring the alcohol and waiting for the flame to do its thing. With his down jacket on and the sound of silence accompanying amazing vistas, Steven is content to simply wait for things to just happen rather than counting down the seconds, confident in a world where he truly feels he belongs.

THREE ESSENTIAL ITEMS

→ Insulated sleeping pad – sleep is massively important, so for this reason I always ensure I have the flattest, most level spot possible

→ Pillow – for the perfect night's sleep, ready for adventuring the day after

→ Alcohol stove – a great way to cook while really thinking about and enjoying the entire food prep process

MOST MEMORABLE DESTINATION

→ Hiking and wild camping in the Himalayan mountain range, being in awe of the majesty of nature

→ If you fancy the idea of a trip to the Himalayas with your tent in tow, then why not also consider planning a camping trip to:
    Great Dividing Range, Australia
    Carpathian Mountains, Central and Eastern Europe
    Ethiopian Highlands, Ethiopia

HARRY WAUDBY

Freshwater fisherman angling for the ultimate camping experience

 @harry.waudby

 UK

 Fox EOS 1-person fishing bivvy

At the age of twenty-nine and having angled for twenty years, it's fair to say that Harry has been caught hook, line and sinker by the fishing bug. What originally started as a means of hanging out with friends away from the watchful eyes of parents has led to Harry camping and fishing in some of the most remote and tranquil places the world has to offer. From the mountainous South Island regions of New Zealand to humid lakes in Cambodia, Harry has taken his small fishing bivvy across the length and breadth of the globe. Now, he spends his weekends travelling through Yorkshire and Nottinghamshire, sharing the land with otters and kingfishers and, more importantly, aiming to pick the perfect spot for the catch of a lifetime.

For Harry, camping enables him to stay in locations further afield from his hometown, allowing for longer drives to exciting fishing spots and the freedom to stay for multiple days as he patiently waits for opportunity to strike. He does his homework before packing the car, however, scouring Google Maps and social media for information on the most populated catch areas. Then, once his fishing bivvy has been erected beside the river, the watercraft begins, identifying which species are dwelling in specific areas and discovering the best means to catch them.

Harry isn't just a seasoned professional, he's also a professional who can be found fishing in all seasons, baiting for barbel during the summer months and picking out predatory pike and perch during the winter. His set-up is relatively simple, comprising of his Fox EOS 1-person fishing bivvy, a 5- or 10-litre water container (1–2 gallons) depending on his stay, a small stove and a sandwich toaster pan which he uses to whip up bacon sandwiches and micro pizzas while watching the sunset reflecting off the dappled surface of the water. He uses a sturdy off-road fishing barrow capable of coping with all kinds of rough terrain to get his camping and fishing equipment from A to B. And when nature calls when he's down by the river, Harry's trusty trowel means he can create the perfect spot for a 'poo with a view' from the shadowy boughs of the trees. Harry isn't the kind of person who you'll find fishing for compliments, but his tent life adventures sound pretty idyllic and tranquil to me.

'Keep hydrated, pack a stocked first aid kit and acquaint yourself with the amazing what3words app, which gives a precise location of where you are anywhere in the world in case of an emergency.'

THREE ESSENTIAL ITEMS

→ Coffee – for keeping on the ball and searching out the big catches

→ Leatherman penknife – for cooking and preparing camp

→ Folding fishing chair – to avoid a numb bum from hours of sitting behind fishing rods

MOST MEMORABLE DESTINATION

→ Cape Reinga, New Zealand. I caught a 7-foot (2-metre) bronze whaler shark during a storm, camping on a beach, a career highlight and a moment I'll never forget.

→ If you like the sound of Harry's stormy fishing escapades in Cape Reinga, then why not consider a camping trip to:
  A Coruña, Spain
  Pigeon Point, California, USA
  Şile, Turkey

HARRY WAUDBY

AMIRA

 @amira_thewanderlust

 UK

Championing diversity in the camping world

 The North Face
Assault 2 Futurelight

These days, Amira can often be found up a mountain or in the heart of the wild, hiking and camping her way across the world and championing diversity as the founder of @the.wanderlust.women. Growing up in an inner-city area in the UK and with a background where being outdoorsy wasn't the norm, it wasn't until later in life, after her divorce, that Amira found her love for the outdoors. Borrowing a tent from her friend's dad and learning on the go at a campsite kickstarted a longing to spend more time in the great outdoors, which eventually led to her moving to the Lake District in 2021.

Learning from the camping school of hard knocks, Amira has honed her set-up and skills through trial and error. After taking everything including the kitchen sink with her on her first trip, she now knows the most important items to bring include water purifying tablets, tick removers and a well-stocked first aid kit. Putting herself out of her comfort zone and confronting the unknown, which encapsulated everything from creepy crawlies to her first time going to the toilet in the wild, she now thrives in a world where the wilderness reflects her personality, a free spirit always searching for new answers in beautiful places that help her to connect with God.

Faith and prayer play a huge part in Amira's life, with her religion teaching the importance of peace, simplicity and mindfulness in a world filled with so many distractions. These notions of zero waste and living with the essentials have helped her with her camping adventures, and the great outdoors allows her to feel at peace with both the world and her true self. Amira must be mindful of cleanliness when on the go; ritual washing is an action that must be carried out before prayer five times a day. She always carries a spray bottle for cleaning her hands, taking care to make sure she is near a water supply at regular intervals.

Amira rightly says that there isn't enough diversity in camping, with many BIPOC campers not being featured in magazines or on social media. If you can't see yourself represented, then it's easy to feel like the community isn't made for you or doesn't want you. Since founding The Wanderlust Women, an organization for under-represented woman primarily from Muslim backgrounds, she has grabbed every opportunity for adventure, heading out with her friend on spontaneous weekend trips and following her heart when it comes to picking places to visit and spots to camp. She now leads other groups of women out on their maiden camping trips, helping them to experience the wild while utilizing the power of hindsight from her own experiences, easing beginners into the world of camping so that they get the most enjoyment out of their time in the wild.

As there aren't many modest clothing options in the camping world, Amira has worked with Trekmates to create a breathable waterproof and windproof niqab and hijab for hiking and other outdoor sports. Seeing a product made specifically for Muslim women in shops and out on the trail will hopefully make others feel more included in the camping world, thanks to Amira taking important steps to making tent life much more accessible to all.

'Enjoy all the unexpected moments. Sometimes things can threaten to ruin your mood, but embrace all the nuances of the journey and learn from every positive and negative.'

THREE ESSENTIAL ITEMS

→ Water – for drinking, cooking and washing before prayer

→ Prayer beads and prayer mat

→ Mini Jetboil – for cooking quickly when hunger calls!

MOST MEMORABLE DESTINATION

→ Lake District, England. This was the first trip I took with my friend Aisha and my first experience of wild camping. The night sky was shining full of stars, and the morning brought the most incredible cloud conversion and sunrise. It was a moment I'll never forget, and I'm lucky enough to live near that spot full time.

→ If you're enticed by the beauty of the Lake District and enjoy hiking in the hills, then consider planning a camping trip to:

Kolsay Lakes, Kazakhstan

Lake District, Northern Patagonia, Chile and Argentina

Tianchi Lake, China

ESSENTIAL ITEMS FOR THE PERFECT WEEKEND CAMPING TRIP

1. PORTABLE BURNER

Lots of campers cook using a Trangia, as they're so lightweight and easy to carry. I much prefer a larger unit with a more powerful flame, like the *Campingaz Camp Bistro 2*. It uses clip-in gas canisters and can boil water for pasta in just a few minutes, making cooking one-pot-meals or toasties in a RidgeMonkey a breeze!

2. POWER PACK

Keeping phones and navigation devices charged on the go is vital if you're heading off-grid. One wrong turn or a change in weather could leave you needing assistance, and mountains don't tend to have many USB sockets kicking around. I've tried many different power packs and the *Anker PowerCore 20100 Power Pack* is the best I've used.

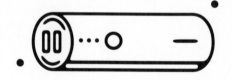

3. WATER FILTER

If there's water on the trail, ditch plastic bottles and take a water filter with you. That way, if you get thirsty, you can successfully fill up from any water source and avoid dehydration. Never leave home without one! I like the *LifeStraw Go Water Filter*.

4. SLEEPING BAG

Even in the hottest places on the earth, the evenings can get incredibly cold. The key to a successful day of adventure is a relaxing night's sleep, which means using a quality sleeping bag that can keep you toasty whenever the temperature plummets. The *Active Era Professional 300 Warm Mummy sleeping bag* will keep you warm and cozy no matter how cold it is.

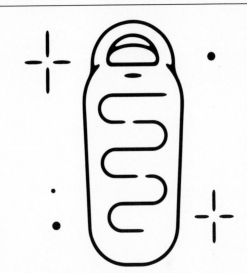

5. CAMPING CHAIRS

After a long day of walking, you'll be thankful of having some comfy chairs to sit in while eating your evening meal and sharing a cold beer with friends. Leave sitting on tree roots to the squirrels and give your back and legs a well-deserved rest. My favourite chair to relax on is the *Kingcamp Moon Chair*.

6. COAT

Walking and camping in cold temperatures can get uncomfortable pretty quickly if you don't have the right gear. It can also be incredibly dangerous to your health, which means you need to wrap up warm when it's cold. I recommend the *Rab Valiance Jacket* which is warm and well made.

4

ADRENALINE JUNKIES

If your idea of camping is a peaceful jaunt in the back garden, then look away now. This section is all about the thrill seekers, the campers among us who run towards the extreme and are itching to take on life's ultimate tests all before we've had our morning cup of tea.

You're about to meet the adventurers who don't just rise to challenges, they create them and set the bar for other campers to beat. Granted, some of them have learned a thing or two about what *not* to do along the way and experienced some near-misses they've been lucky to come back from. But, without their stellar achievements we certainly wouldn't have as many people to look up to when it comes to living life to its fullest.

And as for me, I would have far less cool anecdotes to tell people at parties!

From climbers sleeping on portaledges anchored to a rock face to extreme hikers and adventurers camping in sub-zero conditions, these adrenaline junkies embrace tent life with a vigour that will make you sit back in awe and wonder why you complained about doing the school run or stubbing your toe on the dog's bowl.

Get ready for an injection of adrenaline, and try not to look down!

TIMA DERYAN

Breaking boundaries and contributing to a better world

 @mountaingipsy

 Lebanon

 Doite/Eureka!/The North Face 4 Seasons

For most of Tima's childhood, people told her that her ambitions were too much of a mountain to climb, that women can't do the same difficult tasks as men and that she wasn't powerful enough to achieve her goals. I imagine those same people are at a loss for words now that Tima has become the first Lebanese woman and youngest Arab to summit Everest, making her tally eighteen high-altitude mountains around the world to date. Tima is living proof that a person's gender or background has no correlation to their ability to overcome challenges, and that inner strength and determination should never be underestimated.

It won't surprise you to know that Tima has always chased thrills and adrenaline-surging feats of endurance. From travelling to find the highest bungee jump sites around the world to exploring the world under the ocean and even jumping from a plane over the Dubai desert, Tima has spent years searching for a sport that truly fills her heart with joy, one that might bring the ultimate challenge to truly test her mind and body.

Climbing Everest had been a lifelong dream, and with her sights set on the summit, not even the small chance of success and high fatality rates could sway Tima. Her first expedition saw her camping on Russia's Mount Elbrus in 2016, where she developed a mindset of working with the mountain rather than trying to conquer it, learning to stay confident and focused while gaining knowledge from the wilderness. It is these elements of opening herself up to nature and keeping present that make Tima feel alive.

At 5,360 metres (nearly 17,600 feet) above sea level, Everest base camp might not be everyone's idea of a relaxing campsite. Tima spent a month there acclimatizing for the climb to 8,848 metres (29,029 feet) at the very top of Everest, a process that involved three rotations and a final camp at 7,200 metres (just over 23,600 feet) above sea level alongside the introduction of supplemental oxygen. A cosy tent for a long stay was essential, and her trusty Eureka! tent proved itself brilliantly, with all her gear including two duffle bags and climbing equipment acting as insulation against the tent walls. Tima often spent a week in the same clothes, washing them with soap and drying them in the sun whenever possible. On calmer days, she played host to climbers in her portable home, playing cards and chatting, and when storms powered through the camp, Tima hunkered down with a good book and a hot water bottle

I've enjoyed learning about Tima's story, not just because of the impressive adventures she has undertaken, but because of the unwavering resolve she has shown in overcoming adversity. Climbing and camping on the world's highest mountains has slowly changed her outlook on life. The process has given her a powerful mindset and a free spirit, a sense of courage that she now wants to uncover in others by empowering people through their own life journeys. Through her lifestyle brand, Mountain Gipsy, Tima is seeking to ignite the spirit of adventure in people by the power of nature, adventure and exploration, helping people to climb and work with their own mountains, both physical and metaphorical.

'A quick hack my mother taught me was using white vinegar; not only it is sustainable but it also kills all germs! I used to clean and wipe my tent every week on basecamp with it!'

THREE ESSENTIAL ITEMS

→ Tent

→ Thermal sleeping bag

→ Snacks – climbing is hungry work!

MOST MEMORABLE DESTINATION

→ Ojos Del Salado, the highest active volcano in the world. After summiting the highest mountain in South America, my climbing buddies and I headed to Ojos del Salado base camp. I spent about three days in my tent due to extreme fatigue from the altitude, and we got caught in a snowstorm on the descent.

→ If you fancy climbing and camping on an active volcano, then why not plan a trip to:
  Mount St Helens, Washington State, USA
  Cotopaxi, Ecuador
  Arenal, Costa Rica

TIMA DERYAN

MATTY AND CLARE

 @ getwildmatty

 UK

Seeking pure freedom on two wheels

 Tarptent StratoSpire II

Tent life provides adventurers with shelter at a moment's notice, and for bike packers Matty and Clare, this could mean setting up camp anytime, anywhere. It's this sense of spontaneous adventure that brought the courageous couple together and saw them heading out on a six-month bike-packing trip across the globe, taking in the Australian Outback and the Annapurna Trail in Nepal, all the while camping under the stars in their Tarptent StratoSpire II tent.

While Matty has an unquenchable passion for cycling and has previously cycled and wild camped through twenty different countries, Clare's main cycling experience up to this point had been via commuting as a student. Still, with a yearning for a new type of adventure and oodles of wanderlust, Matty and Clare soon found themselves assembling two bikes in Gibraltar Airport, ready to start the camping trip of a lifetime. Since that day, they have created countless memories while camping with bicycles, turning what was originally a way to save money on extended trips into a way of life steeped with adventure and mystery.

Bike packing as a pair provides the chance to share incredible moments and make memories with a friend or partner, but more importantly, as Matty and Clare will no doubt tell you, it allows for sharing the weight of camping equipment between bikes. The packing process is carried out multiple times before they finally head out on an adventure: pushing a 30-kilogram (66-pound) bike over hills and rocks removes all deliberation when it comes to removing unnecessary items

from your pack, and the pair have become ruthless over the years. With Clare taking charge of the lightweight tarp tent and Matty ferrying the two-person quilt and burner, the couple still find room for one or two creature comforts such as a Kindle, plus Clare's sketchbook and camera for artistically documenting their adventures on route.

In terms of budget, bike camping trips are incredibly affordable. Matty and Clare only saved a few thousand pounds each for their trip through Nepal and Australia. They spent their money wisely

'For anyone camping as a couple long term, we always found it nice to do separate activities for the day when reaching cities and then coming back and talking about what we got up to. We travelled together every day for so long that sometimes it was refreshing to chat about our individual days.'

and worked in New Zealand to afford their return journey home. Their main costs were the odd campsite to wash their limited clothes supply and charge up their tech, and of course, food.

Matty and Clare have to plan ahead when it comes to picking up food while bike packing, scheduling stops at small towns and villages along the way and carrying just enough food to sustain them for the travel periods in-between. For water, they use a gravity-fed water filter, allowing them to quickly obtain water from streams before retreating to the comfort of their tent while the filter does its job.

Regarding safety, Matty and Clare always try to pitch their tent away from prying eyes, though it's not humans that they are wary of when out in the wild. Having previously camped in remote areas in the middle of Spain, the couple shared some hairy moments with the local wildlife, namely a wild boar that clearly didn't take too kindly to them being on its turf. Uninvited guests aside, however, they cherish the empowering feeling of camping in an area that would be otherwise difficult to access, relying on each other to both guide and support themselves through the highs and lows of such arduous but rewarding adventures.

MATTY AND CLARE

THREE ESSENTIAL ITEMS

→ Camera – for documenting our journeys

→ Puffer jacket – when the temperature drops, you'll be thankful for having a warm layer to hand

→ A reliable tent – knowing you have a safe and sturdy base makes for a much more peaceful night's sleep!

MOST MEMORABLE DESTINATION

→ It has to be Nepal because it's such a spiritual place; the stupas, the community spirit, all overshadowed by the biggest mountains in the world. There's a buzz in downtown Kathmandu, it feels like lots of people are about to embark on a serious adventure, some perhaps even to take on Everest.

→ If you want a slice of adventure and like the thought of Nepal and the Annapurna trail, then consider planning a camping trip to:
    The European Divide Trail
    The Colorado Trail, USA
    The Iceland Divide

RUNE

 @risethealps

 Switzerland

 MSR 4-seasons tent

Rise to the challenge

Camping and photography go hand in hand, using a tent as a home-away-from-home while exploring the vast wilderness and providing safe shelter in the most hostile of places. This is an environment where twenty-three-year-old Rune thrives, enjoying the freedom that comes from being in the great outdoors with his friends, chasing the beauty of the golden hour and the promise of the perfect campsite while documenting his travels on social media as @risethealps.

Rune first started his tent life adventures at the age of eighteen, when he headed out into the Swiss Alps with his two-person MSR tent in tow as a means of furthering his passion for photography. When it comes to picking a campsite, the only thing that dictates where he places his tent is the scenery around him, the spot where he feels that he can capture the best-looking photos while basking in the brilliance of nature for a couple of nights. Like most countries around the world, Switzerland has wild camping laws to adhere to, such as gaining permission before camping on private land and staying clear of wildlife areas.

Comprised of three regions, Switzerland has a vast and ever-changing landscape to explore, with September and October being the most opportune months for camping adventures against a backdrop of yellow larches and crystal-clear lakes. As the temperatures plummet, Rune makes sure to check for avalanche warnings before heading out on the trail and he never camps alone, packing touring skis for good measure in case the elements turn against him.

While walking and camping in the great outdoors undoubtedly provides countless mental health benefits, expeditions into snowy peaks may well be enough to send most people's nerves over the edge. Rune, however, allows his anxiety to push him rather than define him; he goes with the flow and trusts his gut when it comes to trying new routes and completing tough climbs. He's the epitome of the phrase 'live for the moment', a person who knows the value of a calculated risk and isn't afraid of challenging himself. And you know what? I think we should all be a little more like Rune, rising to the challenge and facing our anxieties to make the most out of life. Like the ever-shifting elements, life can change so quickly; don't wait around for it to completely pass you by.

'For wild camping in the mountains be sure to check the weather often and bring warm-enough clothes, as everything can change in the space of a few minutes.'

THREE ESSENTIAL ITEMS

→ Stove – for cooking and keeping warm in the mountains

→ Sleeping bag – for a good night's sleep, no matter the temperature

→ LARQ water bottle – for clean water (not an advert – I just love it)

MOST MEMORABLE DESTINATION

→ Adventuring across the Mutschen mountain in the Swiss Prealps. Everything was going fine until we were caught in a snowstorm!

→ If you're intrigued by the Swiss Prealps but fancy leaving the snowstorm behind, then why not consider a trip to:
    Cradle Mountain, Tasmania
    Castle Mountain, Canada
    Tryfan, Wales, UK

LAURA KILLINGBECK

 @laurakillingbeck

 USA

Camping for the arts

 ALPS Mountaineering 1-person tent

If you asked me to describe camping to a stranger, I would start by saying that it's all about pitching a tent among the mud and the leaves, spotting insects and animals rustling just out of sight among the brush and heather and being at home in the wilderness. That's exactly how Laura fell in love with camping, heading out on adventurous trips with her parents, both naturalists who introduced her to the many wonders of the great outdoors from an early age. They ignited a passion within her that would go on to drive Laura to board a bus to Arizona, aged eighteen, to build hiking trails in the mountains as a volunteer, as well as many more wondrous adventures. I spoke to Laura while she was on a 1,770-kilometre (1,100-mile) through-hike along the Florida Trail as she carried her ALPS Mountaineering 1-person tent on her back. Every day she woke to the sounds of the wind in the trees, waving to alligators, snakes and frogs as she journeyed through the wilderness, documenting her journey through social media @laurakillingbeck.

Laura often travels alone, something that so many budding campers are ultimately wary of and the main thing that prevents many hikers from hitting the trail on adventures of their own. She knows all too well that many women have been conditioned to feel incomplete without a partner, and along the way inadvertently taught to interpret independence as loneliness. Yet, from hitchhiking all over the US and sleeping on the streets or under the stars in her tent to walking across Florida alone, Laura doesn't see solitude and loneliness as the same concept. She feels

independent, empowered and whole, confident in her abilities and excited by the unknown.

In the years that have followed that fateful bus journey to Arizona, Laura has cycled from Alaska to San Francisco, around Costa Rica and Iceland, across Colombia, through Ecuador, and around the Eastern US and Canada. She's also worked as a trekking guide in Nicaragua and section-hiked long stretches of the Appalachian trail, as well as hitchhiking across Central America and working as a deck hand on boats in both Mexico and Panama. She is a dab hand at dealing with another aspect of camping that puts many people off – travelling in the wild without access to a bathroom. Leaving the trail to dig a hole with her hiking pole when nature calls is all second nature to her now, burying her business and burning her paper at the next available opportunity. It's all a part of the process and puts her in mind of the little woodland creatures she spent her childhood years discovering.

Laura feels at home in deserts, forests and mountains alike, immersing herself in the inherently individual ecology she finds in each new and exciting location. It's only recently that she has decided to bring a smartphone with GPS along for the ride, previously choosing to go technology free, immersing herself in the moment and making her own routes rather than following a pre-determined course. Still, having a lifeline to the outside world allows Laura to keep up with her writing and freelance work while travelling, balancing her keyboard on a tree stump while creating an income to keep her adventures alive.

'I hope people across the spectrums of gender, race and ability feel empowered to experience nature as a healing force.'

THREE ESSENTIAL ITEMS

→   Steel pot

→   Steel twig stove

→   Steel thermos

MOST MEMORABLE DESTINATION

→   Bike packing Eastern Canada. While cycling I found a botfly lava had hatched into my arm, probably in Central America. I pedalled nearly 1,300 kilometres (800 miles) with 'Spike' poking out of my skin. When he grew big enough, I was able to pull him out with my fingers.

→   If you like the sound of Eastern Canada but aren't keen on travelling with your own botfly, then consider planning a camping trip to:
Finisterre, Spain
Cinque Terra, Italy
Kovalam, India

ERDI YILMAZ

 @erdiyilmaz83

 Turkey

Uncovering the mysteries of the mountains

 Marmot Miwok 3P/The North Face Mountain 25

Of all of nature's treasures, mountain ranges hold the most mystery. It's no wonder that as a young boy, Erdi was fascinated by the secrets hidden by the snowy peaks of the Taurus Mountains, gazing out at their beauty from his bedroom window. As a doctor and lecturer at Uşak University with more than twenty years of camping and hiking experience, Erdi can often be found taking photos in extreme temperatures, challenging himself in those same snowy peaks that he fell in love with as a child, documenting adventures through his social media @erdiyilmaz83 for all to see.

For Erdi, it's snowy, freezing, demanding conditions where he feels most comfortable, summiting peaks of up to 5,000 metres (about 16,500 feet) above sea level to camp and shoot the stunning, secret beauty that one must earn the privilege of seeing.

Erdi picks his equipment according to the weather, choosing between his three-person Marmot Miwok 3P for summer camps and a smaller wind resistant 2-person The North Face Mountain 25 tent for cold, wintry camps. The temperature also dictates what cooking apparatus Erdi packs, opting for the MSR Whisperlite Universal gas stove when the thermometer plummets below -10 °C (14°F). Along with a Ferrino Diablo 1200 sleeping bag capable of keeping him warm in temperatures of -34°C (nearly -30°F), Erdi has no trouble keeping hunger at bay or getting a good night's sleep while the snow is piling up around him. In addition, he knits together snow blocks to prevent icy winds from disrupting his paradise up in the heavens.

Still, like many of us, Erdi learnt the hard way that packing the right equipment is crucial, damaging his left foot due to frostbite in the process. Twenty years later, he still can't feel his toes, a constant reminder that Mother Nature can be both beautiful and ruthless, and that she is a force not to be taken lightly. This hasn't stopped Erdi from camping on all of Turkey's highest mountains however, ticking off Mount Ararat (5,137 metres/16,853 feet), Mount Süphan (4,049 metres/13,284 feet), Mount Erciyes (3,916 metres/12,848 feet) and the Kaçkar Mountains (3,932 metres/12,900 feet) over the years. While fun to traverse, the snow-strewn paths through these mountains sometimes pose difficulties for Erdi, especially while transporting lots of camera equipment across distances of up to 10 kilometres (6 miles). With snowshoes, ice crampons and a 200-litre (44-gallon) snow sled, however, he can safely cross vast areas without having to carry excess weight on his back.

For Erdi's expeditions, it's important to be both physically and mentally prepared for every eventuality. There are some days where the weather is so bad that he cannot leave the tent, choosing instead to stock up on carbohydrate-heavy meals to keep his body topped up, using fuel sparingly in case he has to extend his stay until conditions become safe enough to return home. Some people feel safer and more at home in populated areas with human contact, but Erdi enjoys the simplicity and tranquil nature of deserted areas. Even the threat of wild bears or scorpions doesn't sway his resolve!

'Choose the right equipment
and keep yourself warm!'

THREE ESSENTIAL ITEMS

→ Head torch – for illuminating the camp at night, especially when the weather gets bad

→ Pocket knife – great for everything from opening food packets to cutting through rope

→ Camera – to remember the mountain passes long after the expedition is over

MOST MEMORABLE DESTINATION

→ It has to be the Taurus Mountains, Turkey. I spent my high school years looking at those peaks and worked hard in clubs to be able to climb them. They were my goal and have sparked so many amazing adventures.

→ If the challenge of camping in the Taurus Mountains excited you, then consider planning a camping trip to:
    The Dolomites, Italy
    The Andes, South America
    The Giant Mountains, Czech Republic

ERDI YILMAZ

MARIE-ANDRÉE RACINE

Escaping to the mountains in search of adventure

 @mountain_marie_

 Canada

 The North Face
Triarch 3

Camping on the ground is one thing, but hanging from the side of a mountain on a portaledge while on a climbing expedition literally brings a whole new level to tent life. With easy access to a 700-metre (2,300-feet) cliff that boasts over a thousand routes in her hometown of Squamish, Canada, it's safe to say that Marie is no stranger to climbing, and after managing to sleep on a portaledge double-anchored to the rock face in windy conditions and still getting a restful night's sleep, I'd say she's quite the expert at it too!

Chasing the thrill of mountains and snowboarding back in 2006, Marie moved to Squamish and eventually caught the climbing bug. Never one to back away from jumping into the deep end, her first climb saw her heading to Thailand for a spot of deep-water soloing, and since then she's never looked back. Now, Marie heads out into the wild with her two children on a regular basis, discovering exciting climbing spots across Canada and North America.

For Marie and her family, tent life isn't just a means of staying out in nature for longer periods of time. It's a medium that helps to both encapsulate and enhance their experiences, capturing core moments of their time spent paddle boarding, climbing, hiking and more. With her The North Face Triarch 3 in tow, she and her two sons always have a comfortable place to lay their heads come rain or shine, with the security of knowing that they're safe and sheltered if the elements turn against them.

Of course, climbing trips tend to require a lot of safety gear, which means that Marie's packing process is one of precision and tried-and-tested methods. Her multi-pitch backpack holds her harness, climbing shoes, slings, carabiners, quick draws, cams, nuts, crack gloves, food and water for the day, rescue/first aid kit, emergency bivvy and a small jacket for a cold night on the portaledge, the last two items being added to the list after an unexpected occurrence where that very thing happened.

Adventure is an integral part of Marie's family life, with her two boys liking nothing more than to head out chasing thrills with their mama. From slashing powder on their snowboards in the winter to mountain biking in the summer, they have certainly inherited Marie's love of the extreme. The three are an inseparable unit, a strong team that shares and exudes the same passion for the outdoors in equal measure, a fact that continually fills Marie's heart with joy. As she rightly says, nature is the best playground for kids to reconnect with what truly matters in our world, and what better way to do it than with the world's most adventurous mother?

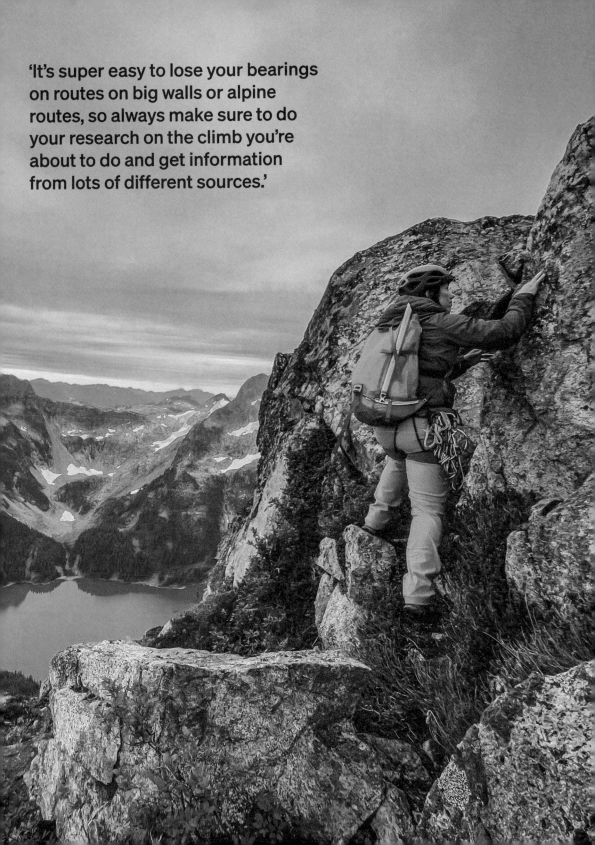

'It's super easy to lose your bearings on routes on big walls or alpine routes, so always make sure to do your research on the climb you're about to do and get information from lots of different sources.'

THREE ESSENTIAL ITEMS

→ My solar lantern – for lighting up the camp at night

→ My puffer jacket – winter or summer, a comfy jacket is always good to have

→ My Hydro Flask water bottle – a sturdy bottle for keeping hydrated on the trail

MOST MEMORABLE DESTINATION

→ Ton Sai Beach in Thailand; I've got to go back again now that I'm a climber

→ If you fancy the idea of climbing and diving down at Ton Sai Beach in Thailand, then why not plan a camping adventure to:
  Les Calanques, South of France
  Acadia National Park, Maine, USA
  Shipwreck Cove, Wales, UK

MARIE-ANDRÉE RACINE

JAYDEEP DEVAKATE

 @hitchhiker_jaydeep

 India

Hitchhiking across India

 Decathlon
4-season tent

Hitchhiking around India is something that many would find an incredibly daunting task, but that's exactly what twenty-one-year-old backpacker and tent life extraordinaire Jaydeep did in a bid to explore the wonderful beauty of his home country. Giving up his college education (something that Jaydeep had difficulty convincing his parents was a worthwhile idea), he has spent the past two years hitchhiking 15,000 kilometres (9,320 miles) across India and Nepal, travelling on a shoestring budget and letting both fate and the kindness of others direct him on his journeys.

For Jaydeep, hitchhiking isn't just a means of getting from A to B on a budget. It's a chance to discover more about the people around him, immersing himself in varying traditions, beliefs, languages and cultures of the people that help him along the road. His longest lift so far has been from Kashmir to the crystal-clear mountain passes of Ladakh, a journey of around 480 kilometres (about 300 miles). By hitchhiking and carpooling with other travellers and road users, Jaydeep is also keeping his emissions to a minimum and travelling in a greener way.

One of Jaydeep's most intrepid expeditions took him to Dras, the second-coldest place on Earth (after Siberia) with temperatures that can get as low as -30°C (-22°F) in the middle of winter. Underprepared for the challenge, Jaydeep very nearly didn't make it out of the trip alive, his tent freezing over after just twenty minutes. With food supplies running dangerously low, luckily a truck driver gave him a lift in the direction of Jammu, saving him from what is undoubtedly a near-death-experience that he won't likely repeat in a hurry. Now, when camping on glaciers throughout Ladakh, he uses a Siyachin -30°C sleeping bag and a four-season tent, a model with more poles and stronger fabrics to make sure he's warm and safe at all times, and enough water so that he doesn't have to resort to eating snow.

If you're looking for a diverse country filled with every type of terrain, then India offers everything you could hope for and more. Jaydeep has had his fair share of camping in extreme conditions, from solo camping in rainy jungles and eating fruit from trees to camel safari expeditions in the desert. One of his favourite spots thus far has been the Thar Desert in Rajasthan, an area where temperatures can reach 50°C (122°F) at the height of summer. Spending a month camping and dancing with the Rajasthani people and diving into a rich world of historical architecture and culture is an experience that will never leave him. It's safe to say that Jaydeep lives his tent life to the max, and that the more outlandish and thrilling the adventure, the better.

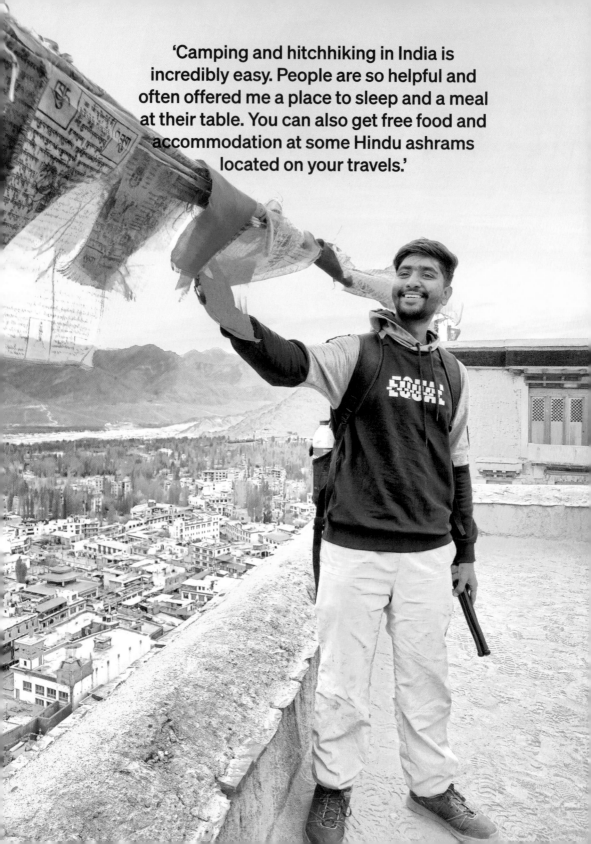

'Camping and hitchhiking in India is incredibly easy. People are so helpful and often offered me a place to sleep and a meal at their table. You can also get free food and accommodation at some Hindu ashrams located on your travels.'

THREE ESSENTIAL ITEMS

→ Warm sleeping bag – for safety and a cosy night's sleep when camping on glaciers

→ Four-season tent – to withstand extreme temperatures in every situation

→ Waterproof boots – because you don't want your feet getting soaked in the snow

MOST MEMORABLE DESTINATION

→ It has to be the Thar Desert. The culture was so rich in Rajasthan and the food was so incredible!

→ If you're intrigued by the deserts of Rajasthan and have researched the correct gear and relevant safety precautions, then why not plan a camping trip to:
    Kalahari Desert, Africa
    Death Valley, USA
    Taklamakan Desert, China

BOCCA

 @bocca_wonderland

 Japan

Championing safety in the mountains

 MSR Advance Pro 2

With more than 70 per cent of the Japanese countryside covered in luscious greenery and dense forests, Bocca certainly isn't short of amazing places to pitch his tent. Travelling between the mountains on foot, feeling alive among the Japanese Alps and connecting with nature every step of the way, he feels at one with the sun, the trail and the animals he encounters, opening both his tent door and his heart to the majesty of nature every morning.

Japan is known for its many mountainous regions and places to escape from the hustle and bustle of fast-paced living, but it's also known for its many earthquakes. Tent life might have initially started as a means of adventure for Bocca, but this compact and often essential means of living is also a means of survival should the worst happen, meaning he and his loved ones always have a way to thrive in the wild.

Although Bocca camps with his wife and family on occasion, he spends a lot of time on the trail on his own. There are times when the anxiety of solo camping creeps up on him, especially when tackling demanding routes by himself. Still, the thought of his loving family waiting for him at home gives him the confidence to continue.

Planning is everything. With strong winds that can take your body heat and tent away with them, and a need to find water for cooking and drinking on the go, Bocca needs to make sure he has the right equipment and plans both his route and pitch site with care. Some 3,000 people get lost in the Japanese mountains every year, which is why Bocca always helps to document his travels by filling in mountaineering reports to give others details of the trails he follows. Despite seeking out adventure, Bocca knows the true value of safety and camps responsibly on his adventures across the length and breadth of the country. Yet despite all his planning and preparation, there are still unforeseen factors, like the sleeping bear he found himself tip-toeing past silently, that can't be accounted for.

As Bocca spends most of his time alone, he usually turns to his trusty lightweight Meteor Lite single-person tent. Camping with others provides a sense of joint excitement and shared memories, but solo adventures heighten both his spirit and mind. They provide a chance to get back to basics while pushing himself safely, all while uncovering the many mysteries of his beautiful country.

'Winter wind takes away more body heat than you can imagine. Consider the fact that sometimes it's safer to cut your hike or camping trip short due to bad weather.'

THREE ESSENTIAL ITEMS

→   Emergency first aid kit – for treating any
    ailments or injuries while out on the trail

→   Gas burner – for boiling up water and cooking
    food on the go

→   Water – for keeping hydrated and
    for cooking with

MOST MEMORABLE DESTINATION

→   The starry sky I saw at Karasawa Cirque in the
    Northern Japanese Alps and the alpenglow
    were memorable. When I got out of the tent, I
    screamed involuntarily.

→   If you like the look of the Karasawa Cirque and
    alpenglow, then consider planning a camping
    trip to:
        Landmannalaugar, Iceland
        Mount Batur, Bali
        Tronador, Southern Andes, Argentina/Chile

STAYING SAFE WHILE CAMPING

1. TELL SOMEONE WHERE YOU'RE HEADING

I know that camping is all about getting away from it all, but leaving your location with family and friends at regular intervals will help if things go wrong on the trail. Make an itinerary and help them understand it before you set off. Consider leaving proposed coordinates for your route too.

2. DON'T SHARE YOUR LOCATION ON SOCIAL MEDIA

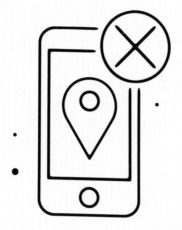

It might seem like a good idea to post where you are so that others can follow in your footsteps, but sharing your location leaves you vulnerable for other campers or people nearby to find where you have pitched your tent. Keep your location to yourself and don't post real-time photos of your journey.

3. BRING A SAT-PHONE

Sat-phones like the Garmin inReach allow you to make calls, download maps and check the weather ahead of schedule so that you can make sure you're totally prepared for any camping trip. A sat-phone will also allow you to contact others in an emergency.

4. DON'T FORGET ABOUT WATER

If you're walking any distance or camping off-grid, you'll need plenty of water. If you can't physically carry enough for your camping trip, make sure to bring water filters like the BeFree filter flask or purifying tablets to make natural water sources safe to drink.

5. DON'T PITCH YOUR TENT TOO CLOSE TO YOUR FIRE

You might want to sleep with your toes by the fire, but polyester and nylon tents are highly flammable. Don't risk it: pitch your tent at least 15 metres (50 feet) from your fire and rely on a suitable sleeping bag to stay warm instead.

5

CONSCIENTIOUS CAMPERS

It's a little clichéd, but the phrase 'take nothing but photos, leave nothing but footprints' has never been more apt than for the contributors in this next section.

Making a conscious effort to keep your environment clean and tidy for future campers isn't just about watching where you're treading or picking up a crisp packet. It's about travelling in an eco-friendly way, sharing rides and hitchhiking instead of adding to the number of cars on the road, using canoes instead of motorized vehicles, and camping in a way that minimizes your effects on the environment around you while not alienating the natural residents of your temporary home. It's about protecting wildlife and leaving all creatures great and small to thrive, all while maintaining areas of natural beauty for future generations to enjoy.

Although you really should be picking up those crips packets too...

Being a conscientious camper also means looking out for other members of the community, reaching out to check on their wellbeing and helping to create an environment where everyone feels safe, secure and welcome.

In other words, we could all do with taking a leaf out of the following contributor's books, don't you think?

FABIOLA STRAUB

 @fabstraub

 Germany

Respecting the law of nature

 Meteor Lite 3
Sierra Designs

Do you remember the first time you were introduced to the great outdoors, the thrill of wild camping and just pitching your tent whenever, wherever you felt like? For Fabiola, her first nervous foray into wild camping was on a joint trip with friends to Southern Bavaria. After getting over the initial shock of going against the grain, since wild camping in Germany is completely forbidden, Fabiola and her friends have extended their tent life adventures through the Alps into Austria, Italy and beyond, even venturing as far out as Iran.

Respecting nature is important to Fabiola; when out on the trail, she feels connected to it, almost a part of it, even, craving the feeling of peace that only comes from being among the birds and woodland animals that draw her back into the wilderness again and again. When she needs a break away from a demanding Law degree, her Meteor Lite 3 tent allows her and her boyfriend to have impromptu adventures at a moment's notice, providing a lightweight, tiny but deceptively spacious and airy home-from-home that boasts beautiful views of their surroundings.

Research plays a big part in Fabiola's adventures, with the German alpine mountain weather forecast app, Bergfex, playing a big part in finding appropriate walking and camping trails. She also spends a lot of time finding pictures of the locations that she will be passing through on her computer, familiarizing herself with the terrain in advance and noting water sources while perusing other recommended routes along the way. It was one such research session

that led to her to discover Mount Damavand, an Iranian volcano standing at a jaw dropping 5,609 metres (just over 18,400 feet) above sea level and the highest peak in Western Asia. As a keen hiker who always strives to make it to the top of every mountain, the challenge was too good an opportunity for Fabiola to miss, and though the landscape and culture made for a unique experience, such an arduous climb with little oxygen pushed her to her very limits.

Even when not camping on the side of a volcano, Fabiola prefers warmer climates than the cold temperatures in the Alps. Still, with an extra-warm sleeping bag and down-insulated boots to keep her toes warm throughout the night, she can sleep soundly even when the thermometer drops below 0°C (32°F). As well as her trusty booties, Fabiola never leaves home without her mobile phone and a first aid kit, vital when camping in remote locations in the mountains where help might not be as easily acquirable. Proper packing is essential for a stress-free camping adventure, allowing Fabiola to return to her studies fresh and motivated to tackle whatever is thrown her way.

'Make sure to check out the trails in advance so that you don't get lost, and never choose a route that's too advanced for your fitness or experience.'

THREE ESSENTIAL ITEMS

→ Chocolate – for keeping your energy up while heading to your camping spot

→ A down jacket – for keeping warm and toasty in the Alps

→ Hot tea – a warming reward for reaching the summit!

MOST MEMORABLE DESTINATION

→ Definitely hiking on Mount Damavand in Iran and the kind people we met along the way. It was an experience I will never forget.

→ If you like the look of the Mount Damavand, then consider planning a camping trip to:
Mount Etna, Sicily, Italy
Sunset Crater, Arizona, USA
Aso-Kuju National Park, Japan

FABIOLA STRAUB

MIKAELA FERGUSON

 @voyageurtripper

 Canada

Canoe camping across Canada and the US

 MSR Hubba Hubba NX

If you stumbled across Mikaela's Instagram account, you certainly wouldn't think that there was ever a point in her life where she didn't love camping. Although getting out into forests and onto lakes in her canoe had always been a part of her life, it wasn't until she began leading canoe camping trips as a camp counsellor that she truly got to grips with tent life, experiencing the outdoors in intimate groups with fellow nature lovers and finally getting to go further afield while discovering Canada's remotest and most hidden gems with her MSR Hubba Hubba NX tent.

For Mikaela, having the chance to introduce children to the world of camping was one of the best aspects of her role as a guide, showing them how to safely set up camps and prepare fires, and how to pick the correct spots to paddle down rapids. She now creates educational resources to prepare new campers for their first outings into the backcountry and relishes the chance to push herself on solo trips, working on routes of increasing difficulty in a bid to continually improve her fitness.

Packing for an expedition varies, depending on whether Mikaela is heading out with her canoe or simply hiking to her destination. Regardless of how she reaches her end point, she always packs her sleeping pad and bag with a pillow, cooking set and two sets of clothing for day and night. With her Garmin inReach, knife, head torch and first aid kit, she's prepared for every eventuality, especially after making sure she's packed all her pre-made food and extra supplies, usually one day extra per five she's away, to make sure that she is fully provisioned.

Having camped in both California and Ontario, Mikaela is a veritable goldmine of knowledge when it comes to the differences between camping in the US and Canada. While Canada feels more remote and vast, California sometimes feels more restricted because of its National Park permit systems. The main difficulty, however, is the lack of areas to find water while out on trails. Carrying water can be a real chore, especially without a

'You'll waste so many weekends trying to get your schedule to line up with everyone else's or there will be trips you want to take that your friends aren't interested in. If you want to get out camping, then get out yourself!'

canoe to help spread the weight, so make sure to account for this if you're travelling with a tent around the Bay Area. In comparison, Canadian trails never rarely stray too far from a water source, meaning you can dip into a stream with a water filter and save those shoulders from carrying excess weight.

Mikaela is a perfect example of how having a community of tent lifers to pass on knowledge to new generations is so crucial, and not just for handing down skills about campfires and

foraging. Her mindful lifestyle, her low-impact method of transport, her willingness to help others overcome their initial quandaries about heading out into the wild are all aspects that we're lucky to have within the tent life movement that should be mirrored in the wider world. I, for one, love the idea of trundling down a river in a canoe rather than hiking with a heavy pack in tow after travelling for miles by car, and hopefully Mikaela will have instilled that same sense of wanderlust in you now too!

MIKAELA VOYAGEUR

THREE ESSENTIAL ITEMS

→ A good sleep system – long trips are only sustainable if you're sleeping well, so I've spent a lot of time building the perfect sleep system for my body

→ Snacks – I need a steady stream of good snacks to keep me fuelled throughout the long days

→ Camera – I wish I'd had a camera for the trips I did when I was younger. Now I don't leave home without one!

MOST MEMORABLE DESTINATION

→ Nunavut, Canada – the Arctic continues to be one of my favourite places in the world

→ If you like the idea of a chilly trip to Nunavut, then consider planning a camping trip to:
Hardangervidda National Park, Norway
Perito Moreno Glacier, Argentina
Rogers Pass, Montana, USA

LEANNA AND BAILEY

Endless adventures with a camper's best friend

 @bailey_theminidoodle

 Canada

 MEC Spark
1-person tent

If you're a little worried about solo hiking or don't fancy being out in the wilderness on your own, then why not take a trail hound along for the ride? Leanna and Bailey have been backpacking together ever since Bailey was old enough to manage long walks and graduating from sleeping in the car to getting used to tent life. Before long, these best friends were heading out into the wilderness for much longer periods; Leanna quit her job and Bailey prepared for life as a furry nomad as they embarked on a three-month road trip through Oregon, Utah and Arizona.

Like many campers, Leanna enjoys the majesty of the mountains and the peaceful silence of the desert, exploring the rock formations she comes across along the way and hopefully broadening Bailey's view of the world around her at the same time. As conscientious campers, they spend a lot of time choosing dog-friendly camping spots and hiking trails using AllTrails and Gaia GPS maps, making sure to check the rules and regulations about when dogs must be on leads on the relevant government or council and provincial park websites.

Of course, camping with a four-legged friend has its challenges, especially when tripping out into the intense heat of the desert or delving into rainy weather. When temperatures rise, Leanna puts a wet bandana on Bailey to keep her cool and tries to hike in the mornings. In the wet weather, keeping her dry and warm on an evening is tough. After a towel dry, she'll usually curl up on an insulated Therm-a-Rest seat pad or snuggle up in Leanna's sleeping bag for warmth.

One of the best bits about camping solo with a dog is still being able to have the freedom to make decisions on the fly and going at your own pace without slowing down a larger group. After packing dog-specific first aid equipment in case Bailey gets too adventurous, which includes a rescue harness, lots of snacks and portioned dog food, Leanna and Bailey are ready to hit the trail.

Compared to some dogs who live their lives wandering around the same block and never getting to see the world, Bailey is experiencing an incredible life thanks to her adventurous owner. Her wagging tail is always a tonic for tired eyes, with both pooch and owner helping each other along when things get tough. No matter the weather or if things become stressful, Bailey's goofy grin reminds Leanna of all the fun this pair have had and how far they have come. Whether camping in the car or in a tent under the stars, nothing else matters as long as they have each other.

'Do some dog training before setting off on your first hike. I slowly got Bailey accustomed to sleeping in the tent by first setting it up inside so she could go in and out as she pleased. Make sure your recall is rock solid too in cases where you come across other wildlife.'

THREE ESSENTIAL ITEMS

→ Garmin inReach – allows me to text and check-in for safety when I have no mobile phone service

→ Dog backpack – Bailey carries items including my snacks/lunch for the day so I don't have to stop to take my own pack off to access food

→ Nalgene bottle – fill with boiling water and cover with a T-shirt (don't burn yourself). Put it in your sleeping bag before you go to bed on extra cold nights

MOST MEMORABLE DESTINATION

→ Mount Assiniboine in Canada – we spent five days camping, and hiked 100 kilometres (more than 60 miles). This is a destination that humans can helicopter into, but because Bailey wasn't allowed on the helicopter we hiked the 30 kilometres (18½ miles) route in!

→ If you like the idea of a long camping trip by a lake with your furry friend, then consider planning a camping trip to:

Lake Plansee, Austria

Crater Lake, Oregon, USA

Attabad Lake, Pakistan

LEANNA AND BAILEY

SO

 @green_blue_black777

 Japan

 Black Diamond Oneshot

Using natural resources and living by the waterfront

Those memories of your first family camping trip, heading out into the great unknown and experiencing the joys of the forest together, testing your skills and uncovering so many new natural treasures, are pretty special. That's exactly what happened to So back in 2007; what started as a trip to keep the younger children in his family occupied soon led to solo camping adventures, and he's had a yearning for the slow life ever since, even changing his job in 2016 to ensure he has more time to spend in nature.

Growing up and working in Japan has meant that So hasn't had far to go to find himself in beautiful landscapes. For him, tent life is a release from the stresses of everyday life, a chance to be alone in a world that doesn't revolve around phone calls and spreadsheets. Nature cleanses his mind and body, dispelling negative energy and allowing him to live a self-satisfied life, something to which we can all aspire.

Rather than delving deep into the undergrowth and disturbing animals in their natural habitat, So regularly frequents a campsite that allows him to feel secluded from the world yet still use natural resources to cook, collect water and live a life of freedom. However, that doesn't stop the local deer population from paying him a visit while sleeping in his hammock under the stars, though they have yet to cook up a meal for him or pitch in with washing the dishes.

So's camping adventures are usually complemented by mouth-watering meals cooked on a simple bonfire. Collecting fallen wood locally, he uses a traditional camp pot cooking set-up, producing ingredients that he brings pre-cut from home to whip up some incredible tasty treats for himself and, sometimes, woodland guests of the two-legged, talking kind.

Carrying water creates an extra unnecessary weight in your pack, which is why So purifies all his water locally using a BeFree purification bottle. It folds away into his pack and when used removes solids, sediment and bacteria from water collected in natural sources, making it safe to both cook with and drink.

Most importantly, So's camping trips have as little impact on the environment as possible. He's ever conscious of the space around him, burning only fallen materials and leaving his space exactly as he found it. Rubbish has no place in nature, and with more tent lifers like So out there setting a great example for us to follow, maybe one day natural spaces will go back to being free of human junk.

'Be conscious of the environment and take your garbage home with you.'

THREE ESSENTIAL ITEMS

→   Knife – for preparing food

→   Fire steel – to make sure that fire is perfect to cook with every time

→   Wisdom – knowing how to look after both yourself and the environment when living away from the city

MOST MEMORABLE DESTINATION

→   The Wakayama Coast, a perfect place where time flows slowly and the sound of the waves melt stress away

→   If you like the sound of a stress-free stay on Japan's Wakayama Coast, then consider planning a camping trip to:
Cape Wrath, Scotland
Milford Sound, New Zealand
Strunjan Nature Reserve, Slovenia

ENIKO

Who needs therapy when you have camping?

 @travelhackergirl

 Hungary/UK

 Big Agnes
Happy Hooligan

Living in harmony with nature provides a refreshing tranquillity that you just can't get anywhere else, and one that money certainly cannot buy. Camping with a subtly coloured tent to blend in with her surroundings, Eniko spends her days drinking from cold streams and foraging for wild berries, exploring the great outdoors throughout both Hungary and the UK. Nature is more than just an area to reside in for Eniko; it's the medium through which she can listen to life, lying in a hammock while experiencing birdsong and spotting the animals that call the forest home. She respects their habitats and never forgets her place as a guest in their domain, observing from a distance but never disturbing their natural processes.

Considerate camping is important to Eniko, something born from being conscientious while out on the trail as a child with her family. She values the freedom that comes from being alone with nature, wholly engrossed in its beauty without any distractions. Before heading out on an adventure, she checks in with community groups to determine the local's attitude towards wild campers, keeping away from the path and camping discreetly off the beaten track with her easy-to-pitch ultra-lightweight Big Agnes Happy Hooligan tent. Eniko only ever camps for one night in each specific location, pitching-up late and leaving early to avoid attracting too much attention.

Sustainable camping isn't hard, so long as you're fully prepared. Eniko lives by the leave no trace principal, carrying her rubbish and burying waste far away from natural water sources. A stunning morning view rightly plays a big part in where she places her tent, but having a water source nearby for filtering cooking and drinking water is a must have, reducing the need to carry excess water in her backpack while heading out for a hike.

From stealth camping in Hungary to navigating the Scottish Highlands, Eniko has spent a lot of time nurturing her mental health through her travels, leaving her worries at the front door and embracing the peaceful serenity that comes from, quite literally, returning to her natural roots.

'Keep things simple! Only take what's necessary for a safe, enjoyable hike and avoid overpacking.'

THREE ESSENTIAL ITEMS

→ Water filter – essential to have access to safe drinking water

→ Satellite communicator – for those really remote areas which have no reception

→ Camera – to document our travels

MOST MEMORABLE DESTINATION

→ Scotland is a wild camping paradise. The locals have a very welcoming attitude towards responsible campers. The country is full of remote, wild areas that have epic views to pitch up a tent. There are also great, free facilities to freshen up on multi-day wild camping adventures.

→ If you like the look of remote camping in the heart of Scotland, then consider planning a camping trip to:
    Mount Rainier, Washington State, USA
    Ama Dablam, Nepal
    Lauterbrunnen, Switzerland

ANN-MARIE

Backcountry camper promoting safety and sustainability

 @its_ann_calling

 Canada

 MSR Elixir/ Klymit Maxfield

A journey of a thousand miles begins with a single step, just like Ann-Marie's very first outdoor adventure when she embarked on her maiden walk in the wilderness. The pull of the outdoors is impossible to ignore, and in no time at all, walks turned to hikes, and hikes turned to researching areas of natural beauty and a longing to immerse herself in the wilderness, chasing waterfalls across Ontario and spending time returning to her purest self.

Ann-Marie and her husband have backpacked and camped all across Western Canada, venturing into Alberta and British Columbia in their bid to disconnect from the outside world. Instead of booking in at a campsite and hooking up to the complimentary Wi-Fi, they delve into the backcountry with either their MSR Elixir or their Klymit Maxfield tent in tow, removing themselves from every stress-inducing device, thought or commitment that bothered them before embarking on their journey.

Organizing a camping trip into the backcountry takes a lot of thought and planning. Ann-Marie first determines how long her hike is going to be before researching the terrain in her chosen location. Before departing, she tells her friends and family of the areas she is heading to and carries a Garmin inReach satellite communicator to check for weather updates and to call for help if needs be. Items such as bear spray are a necessity when moving deeper into the wild, as is keeping food in her dry bag and hanging it out of reach in a tree via a rope and a carabiner a safe distance from her proposed camping spot.

Ann-Marie also makes sure to wash her clothes in scent-free detergents so as not to attract animals while she sleeps.

When it comes to cooking on the go, Ann-Marie has many amazing tips for prospective backcountry campers to follow. Choosing to dehydrate her own food for breakfast, lunch and dinner, she keeps costs down while making sure she's eating healthy food and replenishing all the calories she's used up on her hike. Typically spending two to three days in the wilderness, she plans ahead, packing and dehydrating meals in the run up to her adventures. Like many campers, she finds going to the bathroom in the wilderness incredibly freeing, always choosing a site at least 300 metres (nearly 330 yards) from a water source and where there are no traces of poison ivy or plants that could prickle her in uncomfortable places. When nature calls, she digs a cat hole and covers it over once finished, keeping her hands clean with hand sanitizer to ward off any germs.

Whether beside a bay or atop a mountain, Ann-Marie always sticks to the leave no trace rule. She knows how important it is not to disrupt the wildlife around her, camping where others have camped or using the tent pads in provincial parks to reduce further damage to grass or forest areas. It's thoughtful camping practices like this that will help others to enjoy spaces for much longer and keep the beauty of nature intact for generations to come.

THREE ESSENTIAL ITEMS

→ Knife – for preparing camp and food

→ Hydration/electrolyte tabs – for emergencies
where one of us might become dehydrated

→ Power pack – to make sure our satellite
communicator is always charged up while
off-grid

MOST MEMORABLE DESTINATION

→ Trekking through Alberta's Rockies and
witnessing the beauty of the mountain passes

→ If you like the thought of trekking through
Alberta's Rockies, then why not consider
planning a camping trip to:
Cordillera Blanca, Peru
Meili Snow Mountains, China
Snowy Mountains, Australia

ANN-MARIE

FIVE WAYS TO KEEP A CAMPING SITE CLEAN

2. DIG A HOLE FOR YOUR TOILET

If nature calls, and it undoubtedly will, then make sure you dig a hole to both bury and cover it over with. The general rule of thumb is to dig a hole 15 centimetres (6 inches) deep and at least 60 metres (200 feet/66 yards) away from a water source.

1. BAG YOUR RUBBISH UP AND TAKE IT HOME

The wilderness doesn't come complete with rubbish bins, and the ground certainly isn't a bin either. Bring a black bag with you to take all food waste, toilet tissue and unwanted items home with you.

3. DO A LITTER PICK BEFORE AND AFTER YOU SET UP CAMP

Although everyone should follow the leave no trace mantra, sadly that's not always the case. It pays to be a conscientious camper and tidy a space before you set up camp and before you leave, not just for yourself, but for others that will come after you, and for the local wildlife too.

4. BUY A BEAR-SAFE CONTAINER OR CANISTER

Bears don't know that your food is just for you, especially when you're wandering in and camping on their territory. Keep both you and the bears safe by using a sealed bear-safe container that keeps smells inside.

5. POUR WATER AWAY FROM YOUR TENT

If you're pouring waste water away while cooking or using eco-friendly washing up products, then make sure to do it away from your campsite to avoid treading mud into your tent. Choose different spots each time, so as not to attract animals.

DIRECTORY

BUSINESSES

Active Era – https://activeera.com
Alpkit – https://alpkit.com
Anker – https://www.anker.com
BeFree – https://www.katadyngroup.com
Bialetti – https://www.bialetti.com/ee-en
Campingaz – https://www.campingaz.com
Contact Coffee – https://www.contactcoffee.com
Download Festival – https://downloadfestival.co.uk
Garmin – https://www.garmin.com
Helinox – https://helinox.eu
Hydro Flask – https://www.hydroflask.com
Jetboil – https://www.jetboil.com
Kindle – https://www.amazon.com
KingCamp – https://kingcampoutdoors.co.uk
LARQ – https://www.livelarq.com
Leatherman – https://www.leatherman.co.uk
LifeStraw – https://lifestraw.com
Little Vest
Mountain Gipsy – https://mountaingipsy.com
Nalgene – https://nalgene.com
Nintendo – https://www.nintendo.com
Osprey – https://www.ospreyeurope.com
Rab – https://rab.equipment
SeatoSummit – https://www.seatosummit.co.uk
SwingLine – https://b4adventure.com
Term-A-Rest – https://www.thermarest.com
Trekmates – https://www.trekmates.co.uk
The Wanderlust Women – https://www.thewanderlustwomen.co.uk
UK Bushcraft – https://bushcraft.house
Volvo – https://www.volvocars.com
Woodland Ways – https://www.woodland-ways.co.uk
Yorkshire Tea – https://www.yorkshiretea.co.uk

TENTS

Alps Mountaineering – https://alpsmountaineering.com
Big Agness – https://www.bigagnes.com
Bristol

Black Diamond – https://www.blackdiamondequipment.com
Denali – https://www.denalioutdoors.com
Ferrino – https://www.ferrino.it/en
Fox – https://www.foxint.com
Halfords – https://www.halfords.com
Hilleburg – https://hilleberg.com
Klymit – https://klymit.com
Lanshan – https://3fulgear.com
Marmot – https://www.marmot.eu
MEC – https://www.mec.ca
Meteor Lite – https://sierradesigns.com
MSR – https://www.msrgear.com
OEX – https://oexoutdoor.co.uk
Savotta – https://www.savotta.fi
Tarptent – https://www.tarptent.com
Tentsile – https://www.tentsile.com
The North Face – https://www.thenorthface.co.uk
Vango – https://www.vango.co.uk

TRAVEL REGULATIONS

Canada – https://www.caravanya.com/en/wildcamping-in-north-america/canada
Europe – https://www.caravanya.com/en/wildcamping-in-europe
India – https://www.tripoto.com/india/trips/travel-tips-everything-you-need-to-know-about-camping-in-india-part-1-india-360-5decd1a646353
Japan – https://voyapon.com/guide-to-camping-in-japan
Lebanon – https://wanderingourworld.com/wild-camping-middle-east-rules-legal
National Forest Camping USA – https://www.fs.usda.gov/visit/know-before-you-go/camping
National Park Camping USA – https://www.nps.gov/mora/planyourvisit/upload/Campground-Regulations-Dec18.pdf
South Africa – https://wanderingourworld.com/camping-south-africa

TRAVEL RESOURCES
AllTrails – https://www.alltrails.com
Bergfex – https://www.bergfex.com
Gaia – https://www.gaiagps.com
Google Maps – https://www.googlemaps.com
What3words – https://what3words.com

Wild Camping UK Facebook Page
– https://www.facebook.com/
groups/704669206256645
YouTube – https://www.youtube.com

ACKNOWLEDGEMENTS

Firstly, I would like to thank you for buying a copy of this book. Whether you're reading this in a tent in the Himalayas or on your sofa with a cup of coffee, I hope that the stories in *Tent Life* will inspire you to keep exploring and reaching for even greater heights. Mum and Dad, thank you for persuading Grandma and Grandpa to let me put up a tent in the garden all those years ago and for making my breakfast in the morning. You might not be buying cereal for me anymore, but your constant support in my career means the world to me. Thanks to my cousin Kev Hiscoe for showing me the tent life ropes too, but not for telling me I'd be eaten by a wild boar. Thanks to Brandon Saltalamacchia for giving me a platform to build my writing career on back in 2017 and for that time you moaned incessantly about the tent in Curry Village, Yosemite. Choose your friends wisely, readers. Thank you to Nathan Riley for your superb photography skills and for playing Mario Kart when I need a break. Thank you to Josh Dixon, Lauren Roberts, Ryan Farmery, Kelsey Bolton, and Danny Potts at Adara Tattoo Collective, and to Alex Wood and Chris Dobson at Alpher Instruments for all giving me a creative space to write in. You guys keep me on my toes and never fail to put a smile on my face. Thanks to Alice Graham and John Parton at the Quarto Group, and a special thanks to my editor Charlotte Frost for all the hard work and countless hours you have put into this project. And finally, thank you to all the incredible contributors who have made this book possible; don't forget to invite me on your next camping trip!

The publisher wishes to thank the many inspiring tent lifers from around the world who feature in this book for contributing their stories and providing the reproduced images that accompany their entries, as well as Liam Ashurst for the beautiful illustrations and icons. The images outside of the featured entries (page numbers outlined below) are credited to the following contributors:

Front cover: Martin Hornsey; back cover: (t) Matty Waudby, (m) Brendon Wainwright, (b) Careena Alexis Landriault; p.2 Brendon Wainwright; p.4 Elise McCabe; pp.6, 12, 29–31 James Potter; p.8 Martin Hornsey; p.10–11 Yucca Camp; p.52 Alexis Outdoors; p.80 Chichifusion; pp.92, 93, 95 Nathan Luke Riley; pp.97–99 Daria Shamanaieva; p.114 Erdi Okan Yilmaz; p.154 Ann-Marie Brissett-Laverty.

INDEX

Brimming with creative inspiration, how-to projects, and useful information to enrich your everyday life, quarto.com is a favourite destination for those pursuing their interests and passions.

First published in 2022 by Frances Lincoln, an imprint of
The Quarto Group.
One Triptych Place, London,
SE1 9SH
United Kingdom
T (0)20 7700 6700
www.Quarto.com

A catalogue record for this book is available from the British Library.
ISBN 978-0-7112-6918-7
Ebook ISBN 978-0-7112-6919-4
10 9 8 7 6 5 4 3 2 1

Design by Mariana Sameiro

Printed in China